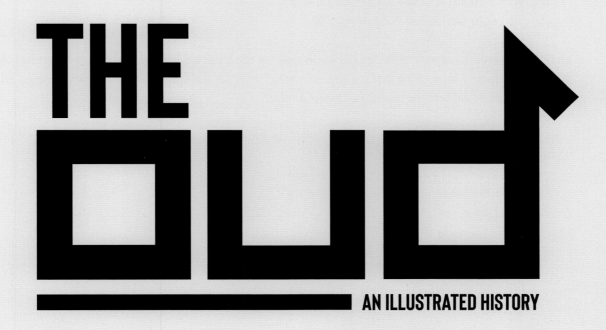

THE OUD

AN ILLUSTRATED HISTORY

RACHEL BECKLES WILLSON

Interlink Books

An imprint of Interlink Publishing Group, Inc.
Northampton, Massachusetts

First published in 2023 by Interlink Books
An imprint of Interlink Publishing Group, Inc.
46 Crosby Street, Northampton, Massachusetts 01060
www.interlinkbooks.com

Library of Congress Cataloging-in-Publication Data available
ISBN-13: 978-1-62371-752-0 (hardback)

Publisher: Michel Moushabeck
Editor: David Klein
Cover design: Harrison Williams
Interior design: Evelyn Tan

Printed and bound in Korea
10 9 8 7 6 5 4 3 2 1

ISMEO

The book was produced with a contribution from Progetto MUR: "Storia, lingue e culture dei paesi asiatici e africani: ricerca scientifica, promozione e divulgazione" CUP B85F21002660001 Il Novissimo Ramusio, 42

LEVERHULME TRUST _____

Research for this book was funded by a Major Research Fellowship from the Leverhulme Trust, 2015-2017.

This book is for Francesco with love.
The oud brought us together.
But it was just the beginning.

CONTENTS

V OUDS ALONG THE ROUTES OF EMPIRE

VI CHANGING OUD REPERTOIRES

VII A MOSAIC OF MOVING OUD-PLAYING CULTURES FROM THE 20TH & 21ST CENTURIES

AFTERWORD

ACKNOWLEDGEMENTS

I would like to thank all the museum curators who allowed me to visit collections and to photograph instruments for study purposes. These include the Royal College of Music in London (UK), the Royal Northern College of Music in Manchester (UK), the Horniman Museum and Gardens in London (UK), the Art Gallery and Museum in Glasgow (UK), the Musical Instruments Museum in Brussels (Belgium), the Ethnological Museum in Berlin (Germany), the National Museum of Musical Instruments in Rome (Italy), the Performing Arts Museum in Stockholm (Sweden).

I also extend thanks to the luthiers who allowed me to visit their workshops and to discuss aspects of oud making. These include Yarob Fadel, Mazdak Ferydooni, Wolfgang Früh, Wissam Jubran, Albert Mansour, Mohamad Aladeeb, Dimitris Rapakousios, Tasos Theodorakis, and John Vergara.

I also express thanks to all oud players, oud collectors, and other musicians who have given their time for conversation and exploration of their instruments. They include Tarek Abdallah, Abir Ayadi, Rihab Azar, Fikhri, Junaid, Omar and Saad Bashir, Kelly Burke, Jack Haas, Attab Haddad, Gary Haggerty, Mohammad Haidar, Iyad Haimour, Francesco Iannuzzelli, Kamilya Jubran, Navid Goldrick, Ahmed Ismail Hussein Hudeidi, Saad Jadir, Abdul Salam Kheir, Christian Moser, Ray Rashid, Dimitris Saragoudas, Christos Tsiamoulis, Fabio Tricomi, Mustafa Said, the late and much-missed Adel Salameh, Walid Shaker, and Azad Zangana.

I would also like to thank all the oud players who have given me lessons over the years. I have never worked in a sustained manner on the oud, and never studied in a consistent way with any teacher. Rather, I have focused on oud playing in bursts of activity during vacations. The list is therefore rather long, so I present it chronologically: Khyam Allami, the late and much-missed Bassam Saba, Ehsam Emam, Necati Çelik, Metmet Bitmez, Yurdal Tokcan, Charbel Rohana, Baha Yetkin, Peppe Frana, and Nehad El Sayed. With particular warmth and gratitude I mention Yasamin Shahhosseini and Negar Bouban, with whom I have studied online during the COVID-19 pandemic, and whose superb teaching and human solidarity on Zoom enabled me to improve my playing substantially.

Learning an instrument is learning a tradition (or multiple traditions), so I would also like to express thanks to musicians with whom I have studied modal (*makam*) musics, in particular

Christos Barbas, Ross Daly, Ömer Erdogdular, Harris Lambrakis, Simon Shaheen and Ali Jihad Racy. And I thank musicians with whom I have worked and performed, right from when I could barely strike the right string to when I could perform in professional environments. You have all helped: Philip Arditti, Merit Ariane, Stavroula Constanti, Atifeh Einali, Yara Salahiddeen, Chrysanthi Gkika, Nilufar Habibian, Khaled Hakim, Michalis Kouloumis, Efren Lopez, Kalia Lyraki, Ciro Montanari, Christine Moore, Michel Moushabeck, Elizabeeth Nott, Maria Rijo Lopes da Cunha, Martin Stokes, Kostas Tsarouchis, Evgenios Voulgaris, and Maya Youssef.

I extend particular thanks to my friend and research collaborator Karim Othman Hassan, with whom I developed a popular online resource about the oud, Oudmigrations [oudmigrations.com]: which is now a reference point for many people. Karim, your conversations both on email and in person have been a constant course of support and also enormous pleasure. I am ever grateful to my friend Nada Elzeer who has been frequently on call to support with expertise on the Arabic language, and generously supported Oudmigrations Arabic [arabic.oudmigrations.com] with her painstaking textual corrections.

My warm gratitude also goes to my former doctoral student and friend Ahmad AlSalhi for many hours of playing music together, the sharing of oud-related stories, illustrations and recordings. I also heartily thank my former doctoral student Salvatore Morra for sharing his own journey of oud discovery with me, including his specialist knowledge of the north African oud world, and his ever-expanding network of interested scholars in Italy in beyond. I offer special thanks also to my friend Nizar Rohana, probably the person who must be "blamed" most of all for my fascination with the oud, given that it was his growing collection of old instruments (and his playing them!) that so captivated my ears when I was researching music in Palestine.

Finally, I thank everyone who I have inadvertently neglected to thank here, and I sincerely apologise for errors and omissions that may remain despite my best efforts.

Fig. 1. Long- and short-necked instruments from central and west Asia.

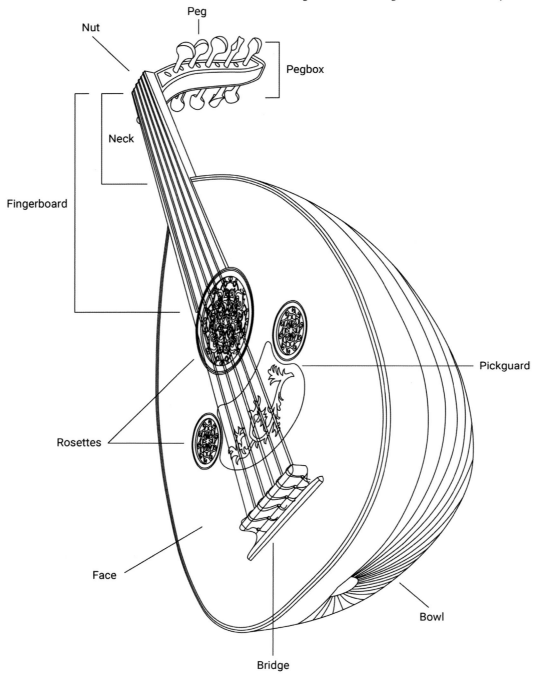

Fig. 2. Line drawing to show main components of an oud.

Peg

Nut

Pegbox

Neck

Fingerboard

Pickguard

Rosettes

Face

Bowl

Bridge

INTRODUCTION

The oud is one of the most important instruments in music cultures of the Middle East and North Africa. Above all, it is associated with the Arab world, but has long contributed to the music of North Africa, Iran, Turkey, and Greece as well. More recently it has spread into East Africa and beyond, to countries throughout Europe, the Americas, China, Australia, and Japan.

Despite the oud's near-global presence, its history is rather elusive. Ignorance and myths shroud it in mystery, and passionate claims about its identity do little to reveal its true origins and its pivotal role in many societies. This book is dedicated to documenting some of the oud's history, discussing its varied construction over time and place, exploring its place in literature, as well as acknowledging its widespread repertoire and immensely diverse players.

I draw here on my research of over a decade among musicians, luthiers, curators, and scholars, in concert halls, museums, libraries, and private homes. My work brings the personal in contact with the scholarly, the musical in touch with the visual, and the past into contrast with the present. The book is built of many short chapters because this instrument has been reproduced millions of times over multiple centuries in diverging cultures and spaces. It generates rich webs of ideas, sounds, and stories. It cannot be contained by a singular narrative.

Let us get an initial taste of its richness by sampling a literary tradition in medieval Iraq about the very first oud of all.

FROM DEATH TO LIFE

The origin of the oud, some writers have said, lies in the grief of Lamak, a descendent of Cain, son of Adam. On the death of his five-year-old son, Lamak hung the boy's limp body on a tree, intending to look at it until it dispersed or he himself died. But as he watched the bones emerging from the withering flesh over time, he had an idea. He took the remaining bones and sinews down and built a musical instrument from them—the oud. He then played it, wept, and sang the first lament. His daughter Sila became a maker of stringed instruments and drums (Grame 1972, 26–27).[1]

We realize that the oud is not just a beautiful pear-shaped box, neck, and strings; rather, it has long been a link to the world of bereavement that allows new voices to be brought to life. The construction of the oud is bound up with longing for the recuperation or transformation of what seems lost. An anonymous Arabic text from the fifteenth century suggests something similar: the ten veins in the legs of a corpse inspired a man to construct the first lute with ten strings (Grame, 27).[2]

These stories have particular poignancy in the current time. The countries with which the oud is most strongly associated—Egypt, Iraq, Lebanon, Palestine, and Syria—have suffered manifold bereavement in the last century. The sheer extent of human wastage, a result of greed and violence, threatens to overwhelm us. How can we witness world leaders sustaining the systematic suppression of people throughout Central and West Asia, and exploiting the dwindling resources of our planet for the benefit of so few? How can we cultivate hope in the future, when corporate capitalism exploits so many on a global scale?

In "Happened at al-Amiriya," a composition by Iraqi oud virtuoso Naseer Shamma, we find ourselves in the middle of this agony. Shamma cradles the oud in his arms at the start, playing delicately frisky melodies. Suddenly he starts to make tremolo sounds, sliding his left hand up and down the fingerboard to imitate sirens. Then he strums the whole oud violently, and lengthily, to indicate bombing. Finally he lets the noise give way to silences, weeping fragments of melody, and a somber conclusion. "Happened in al-Amiriya" commemorates 408 Iraqis killed in a civilian shelter in 1991 during a raid on Baghdad by US forces. It stands more broadly as an expression of grief and horror in the face of contemporary warfare.

Naseer Shamma:
"Happened at al-Amiriya"

Shamma's bleak piece seems to offer less hope than do the ancient stories above, but the act of sharing sorrow through music may give rise to new solidarities and hope. This surely lies behind the presence of the oud in services of shared remembrance today, whether they refer to the recent war in Syria, the ongoing drama of Iraq, or human loss more generally. These events are painful, but by bringing people together, they create opportunities for exchange and the kind of transformation that movement, loss, and song can bring. For me, these encounters form the oud's most important stories today.

Fig. 3. Oud made by Egyptian luthier Abdul Aziz al-Leithi, 1912. From the collection of Ahmad AlSalhi. Photo by Fatemah al-Fadel.

FROM PERSONAL TO MULTIPLE

The story of Lamak connects not only life and death, but also shows how the most personal stories can become shared ones. The literary history of the oud is characterized by this quality because it emerged in a time and place in which human beings felt integrated into a greater system of cosmology, astronomy, mathematics, and astronomy. Arab scholars from the ninth to the nineteenth centuries, including celebrated philosopher Abu Yusuf Yaqub ibn Ishaq al-Kindi (c. 801–873 CE), understood the strings of the oud to be associated with the four seasons, four colors, and the basic elements: earth, air, fire, and water. These same strings were also equivalent to the four "humors" of the human condition: melancholy, phlegm, blood, and bile. The *Ikhwan al-Safa* (Brethren of Purity), a secret society of Muslim philosophers in Basra, advised that the resonances of oud strings had distinct effects and could be beneficial for particular health conditions.

Today, few of us have this elemental sense of our place in the world, but we still describe the oud in terms of a human body, with a face, body, and neck. When we pick it up to play, we embrace it. Perhaps this sense of intimacy has fed the oud's role in literature—it features in the Shahnameh, Iran's epic poem, the 1001 Nights, and novels by authors such as Fatma Aliye and Naguib Mahfouz. Or perhaps its literary presence reflects its aptness for accompanying the human voice, where it supports the unfolding of song and storytelling, not to mention seduction and love.

Personal feelings about the oud run very strong, but they are not just personal; they are inseparable from the political systems that shape our societies. When I first encountered the oud, I was traveling regularly to Palestine for research, and I was simultaneously developing a deep sense of shame, as a British citizen, about the century-long oppression of people in the region. As I made friends with Palestinians and listened to their music and their stories, the oud not only touched me deeply as an instrument, it also came to occupy a space in my mind where the voices of the oppressed resonated, a space that I should, for reasons of respect, not encroach upon. I gradually realized the oud was connected strongly to cultural ownership and male identity; as a female outsider, an English one to boot, I felt reserved about expressing my own perspective.

Nevertheless, I found myself caught up in trying to play it, and then struggling with music-making cultures in which I felt frustratingly unable to be creative. I encountered styles of teaching that felt to me to be about control and domination rather than nurture. I felt subjected to mansplaining regarding what the oud was for, and what Arab and Turkish music were or were not.

When musicians suggested model oud players I should aspire to be like, they were solitary male hero types (usually deceased), few of whom seemed connected to my own sense of the instrument. Ironically, it wasn't unlike being (back) at music college in London or Budapest, where the canon had been created by an array of dead white males. And yet when I played, I sometimes had a sense of being an object of titillation as well, as if the frame of reference for a female oud player was a kind of musician-sex slave.

Fig. 4. Oud by Abdo al-Nahhat, 1919. From the collection of Nizar Rohana.

Now, many years on, I can look back on these experiences with a smile. I have studied numerous oud-playing styles and traditions, from Egyptian and Iraqi to Turkish and Iranian And I have listened to partisan stories galore about ouds and oud playing, many of them sharply disparaging or dismissive of "other" styles of oud, oud playing, and repertoire. But I love them all. So as the author here, my outsider position is my strength. It is what allows me to bring together the multiple voices that make up the history and contemporary life of this extraordinary instrument, and to draw out the fascinating stories of those that have been lost along the way.

FROM STORIES TO BOOK

This book takes us on a journey with an instrument that has existed for about twenty centuries and traveled much of the globe. Readers will find questions answered here about the earliest surviving traces of ouds (Part I), ancient ouds surviving today (Part III), how ouds are made and remade (Part IV), and the music they play (Part VI). They will also gain insights into how the oud is connected to societal patterns (Parts II and IV) and has long been an important travel companion on human journeys (Parts V and VII).

The enormity and diversity of the oud's role in history and society inevitably makes the book selective and personal, even while it is based on scholarly research. A theme that has shaped my selection is migration, coupled with transformation, because I find the instrument's history to be inextricable from journeying and cultural exchange. Without looking at imperialist migration, for example, I could not discuss what is—to the best of my knowledge—the very oldest oud in existence, because although it was made in Egypt, it has been in Brussels, Belgium, since 1839 (Chapter 21). Without looking at global movement, I could not discuss the most influential oud player of the twentieth century, Munir Bashir, whose career initially took off in Europe rather than in his original homeland, Iraq (Chapter 38). It is rarely discussed, but one of the most celebrated heroes of the oud world, movie star Farid al-Atrash, was an immigrant to Egypt, where he made his career despite being an outsider both as a Syrian and a Druze (Chapter 35).

The movement of people is also a key to finding oud stories that otherwise would fall through the cracks of national history. Ouds made by the Qudmany family are a case in point (Chapters 11 and 24). They do not usually get taken up in Arab narratives because the ouds were made for the Istanbul market, but they do not feature in Turkish narratives because the Qudmanys were from Damascus. The Qudmany ouds demonstrate how the centers of empire are often kept alive by human energy migrating from the less privileged peripheries. Arabs from Damascus brought their skills to the Ottoman capital and developed them successfully while enriching the city.

Often the travel of ouds has led to their silencing. Colonial museums in nineteenth- and twentieth-century Europe and North America separated musical instruments from the people playing them. Instruments were objects for display and served to enhance the status of their collectors (Chapters 21–23). Sound was as irrelevant as were the people who had been making it. Many of these instruments are now too fragile and rare for restoration work to be risked, but even if we cannot play them, we can nonetheless bring their stories to life.

If we are lucky, we can hold them, run our hands over their surfaces, peer into their corners and recesses, and sense the aromas of their woods and glues. We may find beautiful labels inside, such as those shown in figure 5. We can compare the instruments with other sources—texts, illustrations—and find witnesses to their crafting traditions where possible. To understand these we need local, regional, and professional expertise, and sometimes we make a few intuitive leaps. Even then, ouds in museums—such as the oldest oud with a label from a member of the Nahhat family dynasty (figure 5a here, and Chapter 22 below)— often present us with more questions than answers. The history of the oud is a history of silences and gaps.

Fig. 5 (c). Rafia Arazi 1919.

Fig. 5. Labels by (a). Yusif al-Nahhat 1878.

The process of research itself becomes its extension, our fascination allowing the instrument to form bridges to other times and communities—even those partially lost.

Ultimately, in this book the oud is never just an oud, but rather a starting point for thinking about musicians and instrument-makers, music, societies, and cultures. The oud belongs to a tapestry of histories, tracing connections, journeys, losses, recoveries, and aspirations. I hope this book can contribute generously to that.

Fig. 5 (d). Jamil George and al-Jawhari.

Part I

WHERE THE HISTORY BEGINS

1. LONG NECKS AND SHORT NECKS

Scholars classify the oud as a chordophone (stringed instrument) of the short-necked type, distinct from long-necked chordophones such as *tanbur*s. The two types are often referred to as "long-necked lute" and "short-necked lute," which relate to the proportions of the neck to the body, and—in some cases—the construction. The earliest short-necked lutes seem to have been made from a single piece of wood, so that the neck was an extension of the body, and the body was sometimes not much wider than the neck. Long-necked lutes on the other hand were formed from two separate basic elements: a small box and a long stick. However, over time, short-necked lutes were made with larger, oval-shaped bodies, and acquired their characteristically "bent" necks. Eventually, they too were made with separate necks.

Surviving sources suggest that the two types also have quite different histories. Long-necked lutes are reliably traced to the Akkadian Empire (2334–2154 BCE), which was located where Iraq is today. It was played for centuries by subsequent empires that occupied the same region later (Hittites, Babylonians, Assyrians). These instruments spread widely, for example, into Anatolia and what is now western Iran in the second millennium BCE, where they increased in size, reaching ca.140 cm in length. There is evidence of them in ancient Egyptian iconography as well (1540–1307 BCE).

Dating from some thousand years later, there are a few long-necked chordophones in ancient Greek art, and the name for them was *pandura*.

Long-necked lutes were also played from the second century BCE in the areas of Central Asia known as Bactria and Ghandara. These comprised parts of today's Uzbekistan, Afghanistan, Tajikistan, and Pakistan, and are precisely the regions where the earliest traces of short-necked lutes emerge, dating to a couple of centuries later. It is anyone's guess as to when these short-necked lutes were first made and played, although it is tempting to try to work it out from some of the surviving sculptures from Bactria and Ghandara—for instance, the one shown in figure 6.

Next Page: Fig. 6. Statue remains from Khalchayan, today's Uzbekistan first/second century BCE. Artist impression of sculpture house at the Institute of Art Studies of the Academy of Sciences of the Republic of Uzbekistan.

This piece was found in Khalchayan, present-day Uzbekistan, which is one of the most important archaeological sites for prehistoric Central Asian art. According to archaeologist Kazim Abdullaev, it dates from the late second century BCE, when the surrounding region was part of a Greco-Bactrian Kingdom, some areas of which had been invaded by a population from northwest China, the Yue-zhi (2015, 63–67). They had taken Bactria (in today's Uzbekistan) from the Hellenistic Seleucids and then expanded their control to take the Northwestern Indian subcontinent. Styles of building and carving from this period and for centuries afterward demonstrate a

fundamental duality: they are Hellenistic (the impact of Hellenistic rule from 334–323 BCE was profound and sustained) but always transformed by the local tribal culture. Abdullaev's view of this lute player is that the style of modeling is Hellenistic, in line with other artifacts in the palace where it was found, but the hairstyle is characteristic of the Yue-zhi, whose first capital is thought to have been at Dalverzin Tepa (Uzbekistan). The Yue-zhi's heyday coincided with the rule of Kanishka, beginning in 127 BCE, which provides us with an approximate date.

Could it be that she was playing a short-necked, oval lute? There is something about the shape, the angle, and the proximity of the instrument to the player's head that makes me want to say that she was.

The Yue-zhi gradually increased control of the region, consolidating what became known as the Kushan Empire, which lasted until a series of Sassanid campaigns weakened it and ultimately wiped it out. The Kushan Empire embraced multiple traditions and incorporated the worship of multiple deities—Greek, Hindu, Buddhist, Zoroastrian, and many others. However, it is Hellenism and Buddhism that most strongly shaped surviving architecture and sculpture, and it is in this context that we find the first clear examples of short-necked lutes in neighboring areas.

Fig. 7. Fragment from the Airtam Frieze, Ghandaran Empire, first/second century CE. The State Hermitage Museum, St. Petersburg. Photograph © The State Hermitage Museum. Photo by Dmitry Sirotkin.

2. BUDDHISM, SNAKE WORSHIP, AND GODDESSES

Figure 7 shows part of a stone frieze from a temple in Gandhara, a region on the Kabul and Swat Rivers of present-day Afghanistan and Pakistan, dated to the time of Kanishka. The temple as a whole, called Airtam, has design features characteristic of the Greco-Roman heritage of the region, but seems to have been constructed for Buddhist veneration of the *nagas* (deities in the form of serpents). The five musicians set between acanthus leaves were located in the hallway of the temple that led toward the *stupa*, the symbolic space of the deity.

The instrument they hold has a narrowing of the body that is more like a guitar than an oud today, but another set of carvings from the same area, shown in figure 8, indicates that there were various types of lute in use. Here a woman is dressed in Hellenistic style and carries an amphora, which in combination with the musicians presents a possible Dionysian celebration. The oud is ovoid, typical of those depicted on numerous later statues in the region. Some of the first scholars working on the subject considered the Airtam musicians to perhaps be symbols of celestial deities; they made an assumption that sculptures of musicians were part of religious ritual—if not Buddhist, then some form of goddess worship.

Recent researchers have taken a different view, pointing out that the life of the Buddha only incorporated musical instruments in particular settings, and in particular ways. It is more likely, they argue, that instrumentalists such as those at Airtam had a decorative function (Invernizzi 1991). We may continue to wonder whether the hallway the frieze decorated could have been filled with the sound of music in its time. Was there a musical ceremony for approaching the *stupa*? How could Dionysian revelry have contributed to Buddhist worship? Perhaps our contemporary categories are not a good fit for practices of this time and place.

Archaeological collections originating in neighboring Bactria and surrounding areas include numerous terracotta statues of female musicians playing ovoid lutes, and scholars working in this region tend to associate them with the numerous goddesses worshipped at the time (Pugačenkova 1992; Hackin 1923; Odette Monod 1966). They can be found today in distant colonial collections—the British Museum, the Hermitage—but also in collections in their countries of origin—museums of Lahore and Lucknow, for example (Islay and Ingholt 1957; Faccenna 1962).

One other strand of the story deserves mention, namely that of the short-necked lute known as *pipa*, apparently used for music played on horseback in China. An early model of this seems to have arrived in the Ghandara region in the second century BCE; the earliest written source refers to its use by "barbarians," and explains its name through the action of moving the hand forward (*pi*) and backward (*pa*), providing a foreign etymology for the word. But the first *pipa*s in Ghandara probably had straight necks rather than the bent necks that are characteristic of the oud (and of later *pipa* models). A source from 629 BCE mentions instruments with "bent necks" arriving *in* China only at the beginning of the fifth century, and it is likely that they came from Ghandara—in contrary motion from the earlier *pipa*s (Picken 1955, 38).

During the fifth century Ghandara had became a battleground between the central Asian Hephthalites and the Sassanids coming from the West. In fact, we have to turn to the Sassanid Empire (224–651 BCE) for more solid traces of the early oud. In Sassanid Persia we find pictures of an instrument shaped similarly to the ovoid lutes carved in Ghandara, made of wood, and known as the *barbut* or *barbat*.

Fig. 8. Frieze fragment from near Airtam, Ghandaran Empire, first/second century CE. Photo credit Mathieu Ravaux; copyright RMN-Grand Palais (MNAAG, Paris).

3. PERSIAN ROYALTY AND THE FIRST OUD HERO

The reign of the Sassanids is the first period of the oud's history that can be traced in writing. Historians Abu al-Fida (also known as Abulfedae) and Abu al-Walid ibn Shihnah, for example, state that the *barbat* was invented during the reign of King Shapur I (241–272 BCE). And Iran's epic poem, the Shahnameh, refers to numerous *barbat* players, including the one known as Barbad, who has become known as the legendary father of Persian music (Ferdowsi 2016).

That said, we are still on very shaky historical ground. Abulfedae and ibn Shihnah wrote about the invention of the *barbat* eleven centuries later! And the Shahnameh, even while drawing on old texts, was compiled and written by Ferdowsi between 977 and 1010 BCE, around three centuries after the Sassanid Empire had fallen to the Arabs. His volume was actually intended to glorify that lost empire.

We have no idea whether the *barbat* was brought to Persia from outside. Barbad's place of birth is also disputed. Some scholars claim it was Jahrom, others argue it was Merv in Khurasan (in today's Turkmenistan), which was on one of the main routes of the Silk Road. It is likely that traveling merchants, even traveling musicians, brought the types of instruments we have seen in sculptures on their journeys. Moreover, it is likely that musical traditions of the time were closely related to one another, while grounded regionally and constantly morphing with the movement.

A reference in the Shahnameh indicates that *barbat*s were brought to Persia in the fifth century CE during the reign of Bahram Gor by a caste known as Lori (pre-Romani). According to this story, no less than 10,000 Lori arrived, all playing *barbat* very well (During 1988)! Notwithstanding the poetic exaggeration, could this movement of story indicate that short-necked lutes were already spread very widely? Or was the term *barbat* being used loosely here, referring here to the long-necked *vina* of India?

Fig. 9. Persian silver bowl, sixth century. The State Hermitage Museum, St. Petersburg. Photograph © The State Hermitage Museum. Photo by Vladimir Terebenin.

Wherever it came from, numerous decorated silver objects from the Sassanid era (224–651 CE) are decorated with images of a *barbat* player. See figure 9 for one example. They reveal that the instrument had become part of a tradition that had less to do with celebrating deities—as suggested by earlier Ghandaran art—and more to do with venerating royalty. Decorative objects of the time tend to represent courtly scenes, apparently intended to glorify singular, worldly rulers.

This earthly hierarchy is reinforced by stories about musicians in their relationships to rulers. Barbad is most renowned from his appearance in the Shahnameh, where his musicianship gains him the favor of the Shah. History idealizes him for this, but the story has an element of brutality. Barbad travels to the region of the court, infiltrates the palace garden, and hides in a tree, captivating the Shah with his music. In his (probably quite drunken) state of astonishment and enthusiasm, the Shah turns on the existing court musician and disparages him viciously (Ferdowsi 2016, 814–16). We may be entertained, but at the same time we may regret that Ferdowsi's tale propagates a way of thinking in which singular musicians are elevated in an extreme manner and then mythologized at the expense of others.

Writer and court musician in Cairo Abu al-Hasan Muhammad ibn al-Hasan (commonly known as Ibn al-Tahhan al-Musiqi, d. ca. 1057), related dramatic stories about musicians under Khusraw II Parviz (who ruled 590-628). The Shah's favored oud player and singer Palhidh reputedly became so jealous of the voice of his student Sharkas that he killed him by throwing him off a high wall (Sawa 2021, 233–34). In turn the Shah threatened to throw Palhidh "under the elephants" but ultimately kept him alive, for the pleasure of *tarab* (an form of ecstasy associated with musical experience). The precarity of life as a musician presumably contributed to lethal rivalries.

Other sources reveal that there was a quasi-official hierarchy among musicians at the Persian court, differentiating between groups of outstanding talent and those with lesser proficiency. Barbad was one of numerous musicians in the "special" category, which also included Ramtin, Bamshad, Azadvar-e Tchangi, and two of Greek origin, Sargash and Nakisa (Miller 1999, 11). What a pity we don't have their stories as well!

4. TRAVELING INSTRUMENTS, TRAVELING NAMES

It is not clear at all when Arab communities took up the oud. From the first millennium CE through the sixth century, they were migrating from the south into the Hijaz. They must have enjoyed a musical culture, likely one closely related to those of other Semitic groups—Assyrians, Phoenicians, Hebrews—with whom they were connected politically and commercially (Farmer 1929).[3] Further north—in the Persian kingdom of al-Hira and the Byzantine court of Ghassan—music may have been more sophisticated, but there was movement between the various communities. For example, the Ghassanid court employed Arab musicians from Mecca (then called Makuraba) from the south. Unfortunately, the numerous Arabic texts from the period do not address music.

However, from the sixth century onward, literary sources suggest that lutes had long been played by the *qaynat* (singular *qiyan*)—literally "singing girls"—in urban centers of the Hijaz. The sources' main themes are the beauty of female singers with their plucked instruments, and the male poets' pleasure in their music. Notable poets who wrote about women singing with lutes were Imru al-Qais (496–544), Abu Khazim al-Asadi (d. 581), and Maymun Ibn Qais al-Asha (d. 625). One of the earliest poetic references is a verse by the latter, where the *barbat* appears alongside *mustaq, wan,* and *sanj*—a wind instrument and two other stringed instruments.

Further historical knowledge of this period can be drawn from somewhat later writings, for example, poetry by al-Nabigha, one of the last poets of the pre-Islamic era, companion of the prophet Muhammad, and by Hassan ibn Thabit (d. 674). We can also consult celebrated writers such as the historian al-Masudi (896–956) and writer, historian, and poet Abu al-Faraj al-Isfahani (897–967). From these and others, we learn that there were singers traveling in the region and that a hedonistic music culture prevailed in cities and towns. Women were in the forefront, now as breadwinners. Many were employed to make music in the households of upper-class Arabs; others were enslaved and sold between the royal courts; and some worked in taverns. Women also provided music for family and tribal festivities, both singing and playing percussion. I will explore the lives of some of these musicians in Chapter 7.

The Arabic name "oud" actually came later to these regions than did oud-like instruments. In pre-Islamic Arabic poetry, the terms *kiran, mizhar,* and *mustajib* referred to early forms of lute (while *mizhar* could also refer to the lyre). Then the term *barbat* entered the Arabic language along with the Persian instrument, which was in time glossed with the name oud, originally meaning "twig," "flexible rod," or "aromatic stick." The names cannot be pinned down precisely, for in early Arabic versions of the Bible, the lyre (in ancient Hebrew *kinnor*) is translated as oud. This slippage between lyre and lute had significance for their poetic interpretation (and the long-standing connection between death and life).

The celebrated scholar Henry George Farmer (1930) suggested the Persian *barbat* had a skin or leather face, and that the name oud referred to the introduction of a wooden one, but Christian Poché (2000) dismissed this theory. Instruments adopted from outside Arabia were often referred to both by their original names and their glosses (the *sanj* was referred to as *wanj*, the *buq* as *qarn*, and the *duff* as *tar*). The terms oud and *barbat* were likewise used synonymously for centuries—at least from the time of polymath Ibn Sina (980–1037) through to the time of historian and historiographer Ibn Khaldun (1332–1406). Throughout this period there were evidently several types of oud in circulation. (We will encounter some descendants of the skin-topped versions in Chapter 27, when we visit Yemen.)

Fig 10. Oud arbi donated to the South Kensington Museum by Ismail Pasha, the khedive of Egypt. Photo credit by David San Millán. Copyright Horniman Museum and Gardens (object number M24.8.56/95).

5. FROM PERSIA TO ARABIA

Our most important literary source for the oud in this transitional period of Arabia is the *Kitab al-Aghani, The Book of Songs*, by al-Isfahani. It is a wonderful source, but we should bear in mind that al-Isfahani wrote it some four centuries later, and probably relied on a chain of (heroic) storytelling for his information.[4] According to his chronology, a key moment was around 684, when the musician Ibn Suraji started playing Arab music on an oud of the Persian style (*oud al-furs*).

Earlier Arab styles of oud probably persisted for some time, but al-Isfahani stated that the Persian instrument became very popular in Baghdad. It must have spread to other urban centers too; Ibn Suraji became one of the chief musicians of Mecca and Medina under al-Walid I (705–715), and al-Walid himself played oud, sang, and composed. The spread of the Persian oud was entangled with the early spread of Islam, when broader musical influences from Persia were enriching courts and also the cities of the Hijaz.

For example, Nashit al-Furs was one of many Persian slaves and singers whose songs were taken up by popular Arab singers of the time, including Tuwais (the first professional musician in Islam), Said Khathir (d. 683), and Azza al-Maila. While they sang Arabic verse to Persian melodies, al-Furs himself studied Arab repertories with Khathir and captivated his Arab listeners with the actual music he had learned. We read that Khathir was the first in Medina to accompany his songs on the oud, but this information is difficult to interpret. Had the oud been used primarily as a solo instrument until then, as Farmer suggests? Poetry contradicts this view.

An earlier traveling performer was poet-singer al-Nadr ibn al-Harith (d. 624), cousin of Muhammad, who learned the oud and some melodies in Hira and played them in Mecca when he returned there at the end of the sixth century. He also introduced a song form called *ghina* to Mecca, and it came to replace another called *nasb*. The story of al-Harith gives us a sense that the oud helps musicians absorb song wherever they carry it—but it tells us nothing about the style of oud he played.

Fig. 11. One of the ealiest writers on the oud, Abu nasr Muhammad ibn Muhammad al-Farabi (ca. 872–951), celebrated on both Iranian and Egyptian postage stamps.

Persian words entered the Arabic language as well: the traveling musician Abu Uthman Said Ibn Misjah (d. ca. 715) may have brought the Persian word for hand, *dastan*, which is used in reference to positions on the neck of the oud and tanbur (we will discuss these positions in Chapter 10). Arabs also adopted Persian names for the strings of the instruments, but this does not mean that there was a standard tuning method for ouds. We cannot even be sure that all ouds had as many as four strings (of this, more in Chapter 12). In seventh-century Iraq, the favored instrument was the tanbur, which had only two strings, and at the time of the Umayyid prince Bishr ibn Marwan (d. 694), one oud at least had two strings, like a Persian tanbur. A floor painting in the desert palace Qasr al-Hayr al-Gharbi (ca. 727) in today's Syria is our earliest surviving image of the oud in the Arab world. See figure 12. The static figures tell us very little about contexts for oud playing, but they indicate that the instrument had a celebrated role among the rich. As I will discuss in Chapter 15, the picture was used as a basis for an *oud* reconstruction project in Germany in the early 1990s.

Fig. 12. Floor painting from Qasr al-Hayr al-Garbi, Syria (c. 727)

6. THE EXPANSION AND SPREAD OF ARAB COURTS

The main distinction between the Persian oud that spread in Arabia (*oud farisi*) and the oud that we know today is the relationship between the body and the neck (Neubauer 1993). The *oud farisi* was carved from a single piece of wood, whereas an oud today has a solid neck constructed separately from the body and attached to it with a wedge construction. The precedent for the separate build had been there for centuries in the long-necked chordophones discussed above, but the shift to this distinct construction of the *oud al-shabbut*, as it was termed, is an indication of vital cultural development that was underway.

From the eighth to the twelfth centuries, Islamic courtly centers rose and thrived in the urban centers of Medina, Kufa, Baghdad, and Rakka, as well as Cordoba (in Spain), and Palermo (in Sicily). Arabia was entering the Golden Age, shaped by the emergence of Arabic

philosophy, now particularly associated with al-Kindi and Abu Nasr Muhammad ibn Muhammad al-Farabi (ca. 872–951), and a broad flourishing of Arab culture. Many historians have suggested that the adaptation of the lute was the result of one player in Baghdad, Mansur al-Zalzal (d. 791). But it seems far-fetched to give the honor to him alone.

There were many inter-Muslim battles and rifts in this period, including the fundamental one that led to the overthrow of Umayyad clan rule in Damascus by the rival Abbasid family, which established itself in Kufa and then Baghdad. But the oud won a new status in this era, particularly by being featured in the scientific writings of al-Kindi (on which I will say more below) and also in its contributions to music making in the courts and in wealthy homes (perhaps in line with Sassanian practices that the Arabs emulated).

Fig. 13. Postage stamps from Algeria, Morocco and Tunisia reveal the long legacy of the Abbasid courts in North Africa.

A figure of particular celebration was Ishaq al-Mawsili (767–850), a musician and slave-trader born into a family of Persian musicians (from al-Rayy, Iran) that had settled in Kufa in Iraq. Al-Mawsili was employed as a musician in the Abbasid court under Harun al-Rashid in Baghdad, then, as the court moved, in Raqqa and al-Rayy. Al-Mawsili appears frequently not only in al-Isfahani's *Book of Songs*, but also in the *1001 Nights*, as an exceptional oud player, singer, and teacher. His theoretical work on music underpins another crucial source about the period, the *Kitab al-Musiqa al-Kabir* (Great Book of Music) by philosopher al-Farabi (870-950).

As we will explore in detail in Chapter 7, musical life at court depended on a large number of female slaves, many of whom not only sang, but played oud. These women were of diverse origins and were trafficked between the various urban cultural hubs. One called Qalam, for instance, was captured in Northern Iberia and sent for training in Medina before being sold to the court in Cordoba, Spain, which had been established by Umayyads that had been deposed in Damascus. Qalam and others lived in a palace area called the House of the Medinese Women, a name reflecting the traditions of where they were trained (Davila 2009a; Reynolds 2008). They were particularly respected for their voices, their composition of songs, and their memory of repertoire. Over time, they may have been trafficked less, as schools for musical training in Medina and Baghdad were rivaled by training possibilities in Cordoba under another celebrated (but controversial) figure, Abu al-Hasan Ali Ibn Nafi—known as Ziryab (789–857).

Ziryab had been a freeman or slave (the details are uncertain) in Baghdad under the Caliph al-Mahdi (775–785) and then at the court of Harun al-Rashid in Rakka (786–809), before a series of adventures and misadventures led him to enslavement in Cordoba. He is often referred to as the musician that added a fifth string to the oud, and philosopher al-Farabi gives him this distinction. But the attribution needs tempering with an awareness of the mythology that has grown up around him (on which I will say more in Chapter 8).

The exact construction of ouds is far from easy to pin down, just as the number of strings is uncertain. The *1001 Nights* refers to at least three types of instrument—Indian, Iraqi, and Syrian—surely reflecting the cosmopolitan hub that Baghdad became under the caliph Harun al-Rashid. Al-Kindi's treatise takes the four strings as fundamental and the fifth one as a possibility, while al-Farabi refers to a sixth one slightly later. On this, more in Chapter 9.

The story of the oud's presence in Southern Europe extends well beyond the traveling women and Ziryab. Peripheral regions, affected by multiple movements, numerous influences, and shifts of power, could display hybrid cultural developments, for which Sicily offers a strong example. For centuries, Byzantine rulers fended off Muslim invasions of Sicily, but they were overcome in 831, and the city of Palermo became the capital of an Islamic emirate. In 909, the Fatimid caliphate in Egypt took it over and ruled it, while Byzantine forces threatened and periodically attacked, until the Fatimids and Byzantines signed a peace treaty in 967. In 1091, the long-running Norman Conquest displaced the Fatimids, placing Palermo under King Roger I. Palermo's Palatine Chapel, built for the Norman King Roger II beginning in 1132, combines Byzantine, Fatimid, and Norman architectural influences (Gramit 1986). There are about thirty-five oud players portrayed on the ceiling (of about 140 musicians), which is an ornamented, vaulted, Islamic-style construction known as *muqarnas*. The musicians, particularly when framed by palms (associated with beneficence), represent the prosperity that the king has brought to the island (Johns 2010, 497, 570.). See figure 15 for one of the oud players.

For Europeans, the presence of the oud was not merely decorative. In Sicily, Roger II's successor, Frederick II, had a predilection for Arab culture and employed Muslim musicians at the court. Palermo was a space of interaction between Christian, Jewish, and Muslim populations. An illustrated manuscript of the *Cantigas de Santa Maria*, a collection of 420 songs with music notated during the reign of Alfonso X of Castile (1221–1284 CE), reveals ouds with nine strings played by women and men. See figure 14.

This era was nonetheless one of mounting papal influence within Europe, making it increasingly hostile toward non-Christians. In 1224, the remaining Muslims were expelled from Sicily, but by then the oud had already spread throughout Italy and, most probably thanks to Frederick's retinue, into southern Germany. By 1491, when the Muslims were banished completely from Spain, the oud was a well-established instrument, usually with four or five courses of strings. It just had some new names, presumably taken from the Arabic al-*oud*: "liuto" in Italian and "Laute" in German.

We will pick up this story in Chapter 17.

Fig. 14. Illustration from the thirteenth century Cantigas de Santa Maria, Castile, Spain, thirteenth century.

Fig. 15. Image from ceiling in the Cappella Palatina, Palermo, Sicily (1130- ca. 1143). Reproduced from Brenk and Chiaramonte (eds.) 2010.

Part II

CONSTRUCTING OUDS, PAST & PRESENT

7. SIZE MATTERS

Ouds come in many shapes and sizes today, as they probably always have, partly because they are often made for particular players. Anyone trying to play the oud knows how the right proportions allow them to play their best. If an oud is too small, the player feels hunched over and their fingers may not be able to pick out the strings cleanly; if it's too big, they will feel overwhelmed by the object in their lap, unable to strike the strings in the right place.

The sound of the oud is made percussively; players usually use a long thin pick to strike down through the strings, and also pull up again. One can be seen in the hand of the player in figure 7 above. Picks may have been made initially from sharpened wood, but both tortoiseshell and eagle feathers can be traced in historical sources and in the Arabic word *risha* (feather). The Persian word *mizrap* is used today in Iran, and also in Turkey (as *mizrab*), but the origin for the term is most likely the Arabic word *midrab* from the verb to hit (*darab*). Today picks are available cheaply in many types of plastic, but some are also made in tortoiseshell and horn as well as feathers. There are legal restrictions on the trade of these materials, just as is the case of some other components of oud construction (woods such as Indian rosewood and semiprecious stones such as mother-of-pearl). Different pick materials, widths, and thicknesses affect the player's agility and sound production significantly. Playing with the fingers is relatively unusual, but some players use their fingers for contrast occasionally within a performance.

Fig. 16. A selection of oud picks (Arabic risha, Persian/ Turkish mizrap/mizrab). Photo by the author.

The oud needs to serve not only the player but also the occasion. In live bands these days it is common to see ouds with cables plugged into them, which carry transduced vibrations to amplifiers as if they were guitars. But when the oud is played in more intimate concerts and treated as an acoustic instrument, the number, quality, and tension of the strings affect the sound quality. Strings may be silk, gut, plastic, metal, or combinations of these, and their material, along with their resonating length and thickness (gauge), affects the pitch they can be wound to, the amount of tension they place on the instrument once tightened to the desired note, and the level of dexterity and resonance the player can achieve.

Measurements for early ouds can be found in three theoretical sources that span some 500 years. The earliest of these is from the ninth century, the *Treatise on Melodies* of al-Kindi; the next trace is in the tenth century, *Rasail Ikhwan al-Safa* (*Epistles of the Brethren of Purity*) that is found in manuscripts dating from 1182–1417); and finally there is a source in Farsi, *Risale kanz al-Tuhaf dar musiqi* (1350). According to both the *Rasail Ikhwan al-Safa* and *Risale kanz al-Tuhaf*, the principle was that the proportions of the main body of the instrument should be in a ratio of 1:2:3, in which the depth was half the width and a third of the length. Measurements provided by al-Kindi diverge slightly, indicating a ratio of 1:2:3,46

(*i.e.,* a longer body). (Neubauer 1993, 293ff.).[5] Nevertheless the ideal ratio of 1:2:3 appears in his measurements for depth, width, and vibrating string length (Beyhom 2020, 156).

These ratios are part of the cultural history of the oud because the authors were building an intellectual tradition influenced by ancient Greek philosophy. Measurements were important for their ideal and symbolic character as much as for their physical reality. According to Pythagorean theory of pitch, the ratio of 3:2 was "pure" while Platonic thought connected mathematical ratios to cosmology, and the "microcosm" of humanity within that. Al-Kindi seems to have been the first to apply these theoretical connections to the oud, but he established a frame of reference that was lasting.

At the same time, realities of construction may have diverged from the ideals, and we should not forget that there were at least two models of oud in circulation—*oud farisi* and *oud al-shabbut*, as described in Chapter 6. These authors were likely describing the older *oud farisi* carved from one piece of wood (see figure 17), although Neubauer (1993, 295) suggests that al-Kindi may have been writing syncretically, to encompass both.

The clearest account of the *oud al-shabbut* comes from fourteenth-century Egypt, and al-Tahhan's *Ilawi al-funun wa salwat al-mahzun* (*Encompasser of the Arts and Consoler of the Grief-Stricken* (Sawa 2021)). Al-Tahhan was a court musician, and his writing is less speculative than that of earlier writers. The oud seems a step toward the ouds we know today, given that the neck is made from a separate piece of wood. But its measurements are not familiar. The body has a depth of 12 "fingers" (24 cm), a width of 16 fingers (32 cm), and a length of 40 fingers (80 cm), i.e., a ratio of 3:4:10. This instrument has a strikingly long, deep body, unlike any others described. And it lacks the ideal ratio. It lacks even the 1:2 ratio between the depth and width that had a long legacy in oud construction.

Sizes and proportions may seem esoteric and uninteresting, but they are important for many practical reasons. The air inside the body of the oud is filled with waves of sound that keep the face vibrating when the strings are struck. So its volume, and the shape of the wood surrounding it, each have a significant impact on the sound of the instrument. Put simply, a big body will be able to make a sound with good "depth," or bass resonances, assuming other factors are equal. But there are usually many factors at play, not only the quality, thickness, and tension of strings, but also the thickness of wood used for the face (which is the vibrating "amplifier"). The length of the strings affects what can be played and depends on the position of the strip of wood to which the strings are tied, often a bridge on the face, and we will look at this in more detail in Chapters 13 and 25.

Illustrations are our primary source for other oud sizes in the ensuing centuries, and these were made in courtly settings in European, Ottoman, and Persian realms. The Cappella Palatina in Palermo represents only *oud farisi*, but this suggests that artists were reproducing the iconic oud image already conventional in Fatimid Egypt—rather than portraying instruments used in Sicily at the time (Johns 2010, 498). Miniature paintings and book illustrations portray ouds being played that seem similar to one another in the wide Mediterranean and west Asian region, although significantly diverging in size. The *shahrud* was a very large oud played in Istanbul, probably tuned an octave down from the standard oud, but it is represented in dimensions that are exaggerated to the point of being comical.

Even theoretical illustrations bring their own complexity. Each of the five surviving copies of *Kanz al-Tuhaf* has drawings that resemble one another but also differ (Tsuge 2013). Some of the illustrations are schematic, some are sketchier. Not only do the forms of the ouds diverge from one another, but the same is true of the string-holders: in some there is a bridge on the face, in the others strings pass over the bridge and are attached to the base of the body. This may be what is indicated in the one shown in figure 17, in which the illustrator is clearly depicting the *oud farisi* model.

THE OUD

44

We have to leap forward a few centuries to find the next set of measurements, and in doing this we also enter a very different intellectual perspective—that of a foreigner in the region. French musician and writer Guillaume André Villoteau (1759–1839) was one of the 159 men comprising Napoleon's "Commission of the Sciences and Arts" accompanying his invasion of Egypt in 1798. Villoteau chose numerous instruments to be brought back to France, including an oud that he measured, described, and illustrated within the monumental, co-authored *Description de l'Égypte,* shown in figure 44 in Chapter 20 (Villoteau 1813). His measurements for the body reveal something proportionately shorter and wider than that of al-Tahhan: 162 mm (depth), 350 mm (width), and 433 mm (length), i.e., proportions corresponding to a ratio of 1:2.1:2.67. The neck is 224 mm in length. However, as Tarek Abdallah has noted (2017, 110ff.; 2016), Villoteau's measurements do not quite add up, so it is possible that the length was greater (he proposes 453 mm), making the proportions 1:2.1:2.79.

As mentioned at the beginning of this chapter, all these seemingly abstract measurements become crucial when anyone picks up an oud to play it. The oud must fit the body of the player and be comfortably manageable for the types of music that will be played. In the end, the player of the oud needs to feel like it is an extension of their body, as it seems from photos of Iraqi virtuoso Jamil Bashir (1920–1977) playing his oud. These reveal that he cultivated a very intense physical relationship with his instrument. He often turned in to it and curved his back, or drew it up high toward his face, even lifting the neck to make the oud slant unusually steeply.

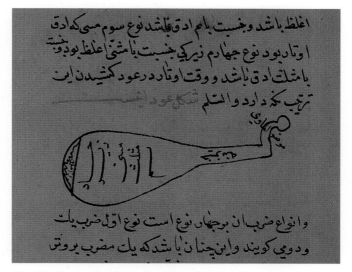

Fig. 17. Illustration from the Kanz al-Tuhaf. Courtesy of the National Library of France, Persian Supplement 1121 f.173v.

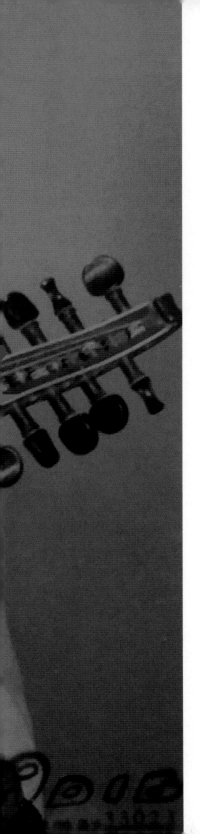

Crucially, for the virtuoso that he was, his instrument was smaller than most Arab instruments of the time (although the face is relatively wide in comparison to the depth, namely 37 cm/17.5 cm). The length of the vibrating part of the string is relatively short at 58.5 cm, so it is more manageable for showpieces than the Arab length that was then typical (at least 60 cm). The fingerboard extending onto the face was an innovation that became necessary from the 1920s onward, as players started to use an increasingly extended range. (We will explore this change in Chapter 31.)

Bashir's main instrument was made by the celebrated Usta Ali a.k.a. Ali Khanbaba (1904–1960) and his son Muhammad Ali (1930–2002) (Beckles Willson and Othman Hassan 2017). The workshop of these luthiers was an established supplier for Baghdad's oud virtuosi from the 1930s onward. By the time his instrument was made in the 1950s (the label of 1956 may refer to a repair), Bashir was a leading figure among these musicians. Othman Hassan identifies the body as made of twenty-one finely worked rosewood (*Dalbergia*) strips, separated most probably by maple. The oud is very

light, so the rather heavy wood must have been cut very thin. Today the trend toward smaller instruments can be traced in the institutionalized oud model of Beit al-Oud in Cairo, an institute for oud study founded in 1998 by the Iraqi Naseer Shamma (again, of this more in Chapter 31). The strings made at Beit al-Oud have a vibrating string length of just 57 cm, which bring the nimble moves of fashionable contemporary virtuosity more within reach.

Egyptian musician and researcher Mustafa Said offers a very different perspective on oud sizes today. Beyond his work as an oud player, a singer, and composer, and his work on recovering historical recordings, Said founded the Asil Ensemble, which included three oud of different sizes, tuned one octave apart from one another, to contribute to different areas of resonance in the group (Asīl Ensemble and Said 2010). His starting point for working out the sizes was his own left hand on the neck and the degree of extension (for the largest oud) and compression (for the smallest) that was going to be comfortable. These dimensions had to be reconciled with strings that could be of the right tension and gauges to reach the right pitches.

Fig. 18. Jamil Bashir. Courtesy of Junaid Bashir.

8. MAKING OUD BODIES

Since the earliest writing about ouds, as we have seen, there has been a temptation to think about them anthropomorphically: they have a neck, a face, and a body. They may even shed tears, such as in cartoons of movie star oud player Farid al-Atrash, or in the *1001 Nights* when they lament their lost lives as trees. Related instruments are thought about in the same way: the Turkish *saz* is said to laugh and cry (Bates 2012) and the guitar may weep too (in the Beatles' "While My Guitar Gently Weeps"). There is a visual element as well; once a player is wrapped around an oud and curved toward it to play, her own torso, face, and neck may be largely obscured, as if her own body is translated into the body, face, and neck of the instrument.

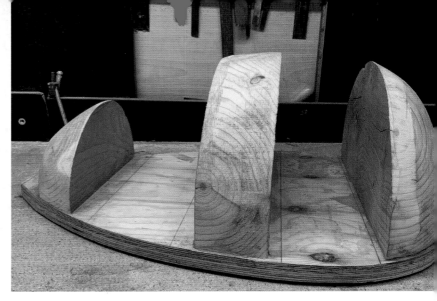

Fig. 19. Sample oud mold. Workshop of Mohamad Aladeeb.

Since at least the time of al-Kindi, the vaulted body of the oud has been made from strips of hardwood, curved from the base as if into a half sphere but tapering toward the neck joint. Al-Tahhan noted eleven of these strips (or "ribs"), sometimes thirteen. Both the ribs and the face were made of cypress, he wrote, whereas *Kanz al-Tuhaf* mentioned cedar brought by sea to Persia (probably from Lebanon or India).

An extravagant alternative was agarwood from India, which was also used for decorations—as were sandalwood, camphorwood, gold, precious stones, ivory, and ebony, according to al-Tahhan. Over subsequent centuries a diverse range of woods has been used for different parts of the instrument, including walnut, hawthorn, larch, beech, acorn, pistachio, oak, mahogany, and spruce.

The actual methods of transforming thin strips of wood into a beautifully shaped bowl almost always depend today on the existence of a mold. (A notable exception is the work of Albert Mansur in Beirut.) Bowls are frequently mass-produced today, serving mass demand and enabling some luthiers to concentrate on the face and other parts, and sell instruments at lower prices. But many luthiers working by hand make their own molds and then reuse them many times, basing them on measurements of the desired string length, length, depth, and width of the instrument.

When an oud is made, blocks are attached to either end of the mold and shaped so they can become integral inner parts of the instrument. The mold can be marked to delineate the even spacing of the ribs. Wood strips are made to curve over a hot iron bending mold and planed to taper at each end. The first is placed over the center of the mold, hide glue is used to secure it to each block, and it may also be pinned to the mold while the glue dries.

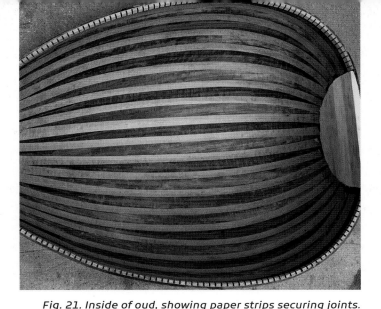

Fig. 21. Inside of oud, showing paper strips securing joints. Workshop of Mohamad Aladeeb.

Fig. 20. Bending mold for ribs. Workshop of Mohamad Aladeeb.

Once the glue is set (hide glue dries quickly when heat is applied), the second and third strips can be placed alongside it, already planed to ensure a tight fit, and then planed on their external edge to the right size at every point of their tapering length. Often a thin strip of wood ("purfling"), usually of a contrasting color, is inserted between the ribs. Hot glue is applied to the blocks and to the edges of the purfling. The glue is set by a hot iron applied to strips or squares of paper placed along the length, after which temporarily inserted pins can be removed. Today ouds are frequently made from twenty-one or twenty-three ribs. Once they are all secured, the bowl can be removed from the mold and rubbed clean, and paper or linen strips are glued inside the instrument to further secure the joints.

The face, made from two or three pieces of thinly planed hardwood, is furnished with wooden bars known as braces inside, positioned in places that are crucial for the resonance (see figure 22). Resonance holes are cut out from the face, and a bridge is glued on, allowing the strings attached to it to be tightened to the desired length. According to al-Kindi, this bridge should be at a distance from the base of the bowl that is one-sixth of the length from the base to the nut. In other words, an oud that is thirty-six fingers long should have a bridge secured six fingers from the edge of the bowl and the resonating section of the string should be thirty fingers long. The bridge conducts the vibrations of the strings to the face of the oud, so its consistency and position are both fundamental. Al-Tahhan notes that the bridge should not be "burdened" by decorations, which could deaden the sound (Neubauer 1993, 285). A pickguard stuck on the face just inside the bridge protects the face at the most resonant place for picking.

The neck (generally approximately a third of the resonant section of the string) is attached to the block, often with a dowel, just as the tapering pegbox is attached to the end of the neck. The face is glued onto the bowl, and at times the join is reinforced by a fabric strip around the outside or at the base of the bowl. A thin piece of wood is laid on top of the neck as the fingerboard.

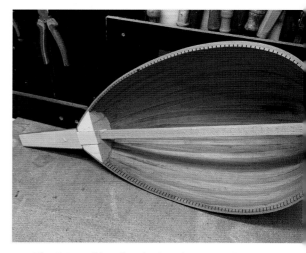

Fig. 23. Inside of oud, showing neckpiece inserted. (Bracing post is removed once the soundboard is attached.) Workshop of Mohamad Aladeeb.

Fig. 22. Inner soundboard of oud, showing resonance bars and Mohamad Aladeeb demonstrating his tuning process. Workshop of Mohamad Aladeeb.

For some centuries it seems the face extended onto the neck to meet the fingerboard after the join. During the nineteenth century in Syria this changed; the fingerboard stopped at the join, and a decorative figure known as a "luiza" was laid on. During the twentieth century, the fingerboard was extended progressively to the main sound hole, supporting the increasing interest in playing in high registers.

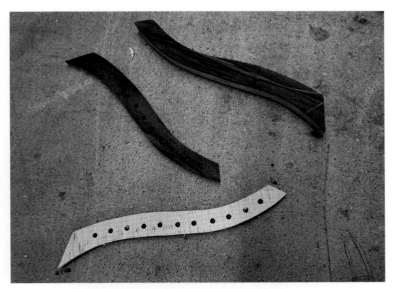

Fig. 24 (b) Neckpieces. Workshop of Mohamad Aladeeb.

Fig. 24 (a) Pegbox. Workshop of Mohamad Aladeeb

Ouds offer numerous opportunities for decoration, including the back, the pickguard, and the fingerboard. Decorative woods are used as veneers, such as rosewoods, amboyna, pau ferro and makore (see figure 25), but the rosettes inserted into the resonance holes are the most obvious. Many rosettes from the nineteenth and twentieth centuries are carved from bone, although many are made of wood. They may include calligraphy and songbirds, or delicate arabesque or geometrical patterns. Some flashy ouds have rosettes surrounded by inlays of (usually fake) mother-of-pearl, which may also be present on the fingerboard. The example of the celebrated musician Farid al-Atrash popularized the style in twentieth-century Egypt.

Fig. 25. Wood sheets for veneer. Workshop of Mohamad Aladeeb.

The various shapes of bowl have varied over the centuries and regions, as luthiers have attempted to improve ergonomics and type of sound. In one recent innovation shown below in figure 27a, luthier Sebastian Stenzl made an oud that is less wide and less deep than is usual but compensates for the loss of air volume (and thus bass resonance) with an expanded body that swells beyond the face. He also reverted to the earlier use of only eleven ribs, maximizing the individual resonance set off by each of these slightly concave surfaces inside. The model necessitated a mold that could come apart in two pieces when the oud was formed.

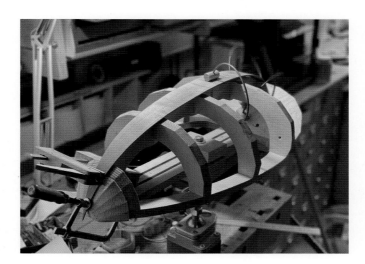

Fig. 27a Oud mold by Sebastian Stenzl (2019).

Figs. 26a-f. Rosettes made by (a) Rafia Arazi in 1919 (b) Abdo al-Nahhat in 1917 (c) Abdo al-Nahhat in 1919 (d) al-Jawhari in 1935 (e) al-Jawhari in 1946 (f) Ikhwan al-Nahhat in 1899

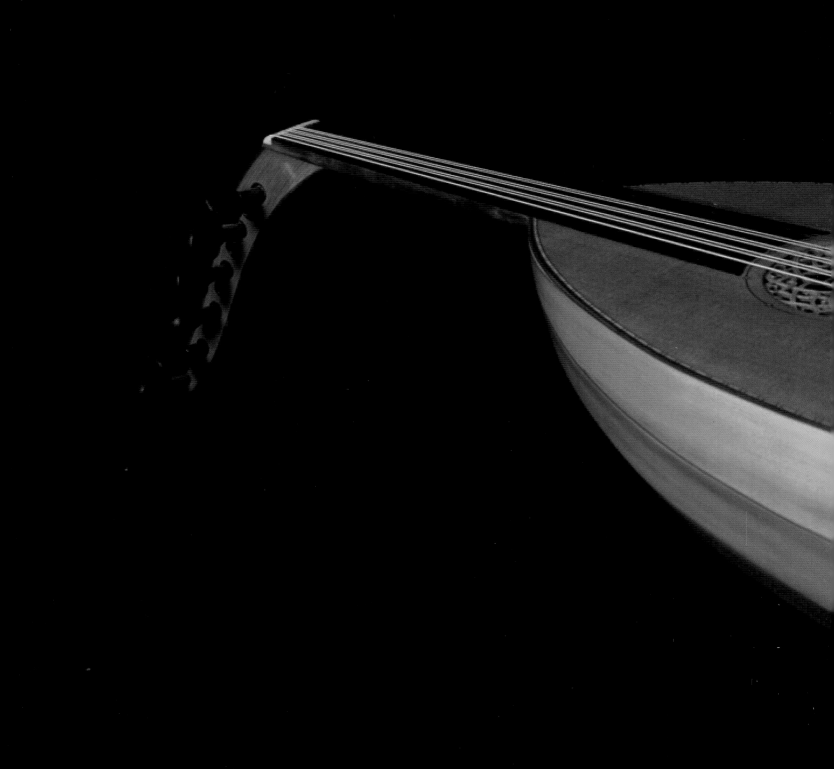

Fig. 27 (b) new oud model by Sebastian Stenzl (2019)

9. STRINGING THE OUD

Oud strings at the time of al-Kindi were as colorful as the symbolism associated with them. The standard four double courses were black, white, red, and yellow, and they were understood as corresponding to bodily fluids, or humors, expounded by Aristotle: black bile, white phlegm, red blood, and yellow bile (Neubauer 1993, 319). These, in turn, had cosmic correlates—earth, water, air, and fire. The *Ikhwan* explained human beings as "microcosms" of the universe, which was a "macro-anthropos" (Wright 2010, xviii). The syncretic scheme may have been part of an attempt to transcend the sectarianism of the time in which they lived.

Al-Kindi and the *Ikhwan*, as well as many other writers in Arabic, Persian, and Turkish, consequently claimed that the sound of oud strings could be employed therapeutically.

According to the *Ikhwan*:

> *When these notes are combined in rhythmic melodies [alhan] corresponding [mushakila] to them, and these melodies are then used at the times of day or night whose nature is counter to that of the prevailing illnesses and sicknesses occurring, they will alleviate them, reduce their severity, and ease the pain they inflict on the sick, because when things that correspond in their characteristics are multiplied and combined, their effects become more powerful and their influence prevails, overcoming their opposites-just as people realize during wars and disputes.* (Wright 2010, 129–30)

This early "music therapy" built on four material qualities—cold, moisture, dryness, and heat—that could be used in combination with climate to explain and transform human temperaments. Overly heavy humors (cold and wet) could be counteracted by the sounds of the upper (dry, hot) strings, and vice versa, with middle-range sounds supporting an overall balance between sanguine, choleric, melancholy, and phlegmatic humors. Medical understanding changed over time, but string coloring originally linked with them continued for many centuries and across continents. The Persian names for strings adopted by the Arabs were—in ascending pitch—*bamm*, *matlat*, *mathna*, and *zir*. Since at least the time of al-Tahhan, the courses have been double, and during al-Tahhan's life in eleventh-century Cairo, there were generally four double courses of strings. Nevertheless, he knew of the existence of instruments with five double courses elsewhere. Al-Kindi mentioned the possibility of a fifth course as well, while numerous writers commenting on Iraq and North Africa indicate that the standard remained four. The philosopher al-Farabi referred to this possible fifth course *hadd*, reinforcing earlier writers' indications that it extended the range upward. However, the legendary musician Ziryab is said to have incorporated a fifth, central course, and dyed it red like the *mathna*. This one was associated with the soul as well.

Fig. 28. Image from ceiling in the Cappella Palatina, Palermo, Sicily (1130- ca. 1143). Courtesy of the Ministero per i beni culturali, Italy.

The resulting five-course instrument had become established in Persia by the end of the thirteenth century CE, as indicated by *Kanz al-Tuhaf*, and numerous writers including Safi al-Din Abd al-Mumin ibn Yusuf ibn al-Fakhir al-Urmawi al-Baghdadi (born ca. 1216 in Urmia, died in 1294 in Baghdad). Foremost court musician and composer in Persia Abd al-Qadir al-Maraghi bin Ghaybi (d. 1435) identified it as an improvement on the four-course instrument, naming the two *oud e-qadim* and *oud e-kamal*, respectively. It was also increasingly admired and played elsewhere (Othman Hassan 2016e; Neubauer 1993, 308). Figure 28 shows it was known by painters of the Cappella Palatina in Sicily, who were probably from Fatimid Egypt, even while the same Cappella ceiling features four-course instruments as well, as shown in figure 13 above.

Within a few years, a further course was coming into use in Ottoman Turkey, as we can trace in the writing of Muhammad ibn Abd al-Hamid al-Ladiqi (d. after 1485). Al-Ladiqi attributed the resulting *oud akmal* (the most perfect oud) to the oldest son of Maraghi. The nephew of this son, a musician at the Ottoman court, is associated with the next step, namely a seven-course instrument, which he referred to as the *oud mukmal* (the extended oud) (Neubauer 1993, 308). This seven-course instrument must have spread outward from Istanbul, although as we will see, a six-course instrument remained in existence alongside it in Egypt and elsewhere for several centuries.

The materials used to construct and color these strings are worth a moment's thought. From al-Kindi onward, the tendency was to use gut for the two lowest courses and silk for the upper ones. The use of silk for stringed instruments probably stretched back even beyond Persia into Ghandara. *Kanz al-Tuhaf* details not only the number of silk threads for the different string weights (from 64 for the *bamm* to 16 for the *zir*), but the selection of silk and its polishing, washing, and drying. Sheep gut was used for the lower strings, with ewe recommended over ram. Dying materials include saffron and poppy juice. The thickness of all these strings was decisive in terms of the tension to which they could be stretched and the pitch at which they could most effectively resonate.

What pitch these ouds were played at remains somewhat speculative, although the relationships between them are quite clear. Al-Kindi suggests beginning with the lowest note of a singing human for the *bamm* and building upward in fourths. (Setting aside the important distinction between "just" and "equal" temperament, this is as today.[6]) The *Ikhwan* take the opposite approach, starting with the maximum tension of a *zir* string and moving downward in fourths. But this is leading us into the actual stringing of the oud, and in order to consider that we need to look further at the construction of the instrument, and in particular its frets.

10. TUNING AND FRETTING

There is a range of oud tunings in existence today, but one quirky tradition unifies them all. When players check and adjust their strings, they start not with the first or last one, but with the second from the right (on a standard Arab oud today this is a G), before moving to the right (C) and then to the left for D, A, and so on. Why? Because they have been taught to do this. Along with their teachers, they are (unknowingly) perpetuating a tradition that stems from court ensemble players in the time of the khalifs; musicians knew the second oud string as the "support" note (*imad*) and tuned it first (Neubauer 1993, 321).

The oldest tuning known to be used for lutes in the Arab world had the two lowest strings in pitch tuned one tone apart from each other, with a gap of a fourth before the two upper strings, which were also one tone apart. Once a player put their fingers on them, the range of just one octave could be played in the basic position. This was overtaken by the system already in use in Persia, in which the courses of strings were one fourth apart. But the second string, the *imad* of the time of the khalifs, was unlikely to be the G of today, because the strings were arranged on the oud in an overlapping pitch pattern, rather than the linear one that has become standard now. Whereas today we are used to a sequence of *bamm, mathlath, mathna,* and *zir* for strings IV, III, II, I, the overlapping arrangement was *mathna, zir, mathlath, bamm* (II, I, III, IV).

One textual source reveals a linear arrangement was used for a seven-course *oud mukmal* in Cairo in the fourteenth century, but this was a scale—like that of a harp—rather than a series of fourths, and it is unlikely to have been used extensively (Franke and Neubauer, 2000, 12). Today's completely linear arrangement of fourths may in fact be a rather recent development in terms of the long history of the oud. Even the instrument as illustrated by Villoteau reveals an overlapping of pitches for its seven strings (see figure 30). Distinctions between string arrangements are likely to have been regional as well.

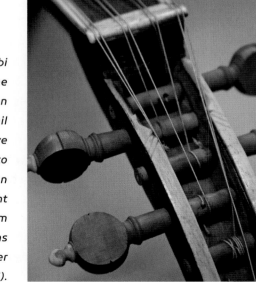

Fig. 29. Oud arbi donated to the South Kensington Museum by Ismail Pasha, the khedive of Egypt. Photo credit by David San Millán. Copyright Horniman Museum and Gardens (object number M24.8.56/95).

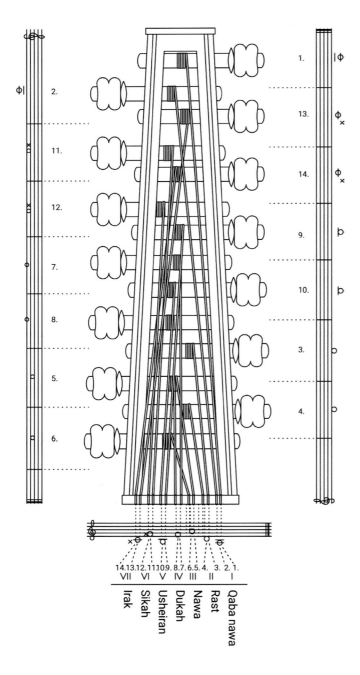

Fig. 30. Redrawing of Villoteau's indication of stringing.
Description de l'Égypte, État moderne, Volume XIII, p. 238.

At the turn of the twentieth century in Istanbul, some players kept a single *bamm* string on the right, while lining up all other double courses. In this arrangement the lowest note in pitch is beside the highest. From photos of Udi Hrant Kenkulian (1901–1978) and Sherif Muhiddin Targan (1892–1967), each of whom spent much of his life in Istanbul, it is easy to see the single *bamm* string is on the lower end (right side) of the instrument, whereas all the others are double courses. When Sherif Muhiddin moved to Iraq in 1935, he probably carried this string arrangement with him on his oud. The celebrated oud virtuosi of Iraq, Jamil and Munir Bashir, tuned their instruments in the same way, as can be traced precisely not only in photos but in but in Jamil's oud-playing tutorial, published in 1961 (see Chapter 31 for more about Jamil).

Fig. 31. Extract from Jamil Bashir's Oud method (J. Bashir 1961a).

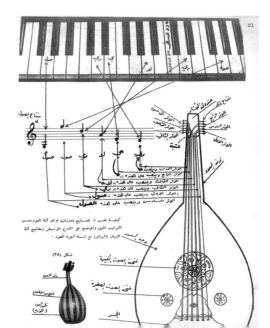

For players today, electronic tuners following standardized agreements about pitch make it a relatively straightforward process to tune each string individually according to "equal temperament," the system of tuning that came to dominate industrially produced instruments worldwide during the nineteenth century. Both al-Kindi and ibn al-Tahhan, on the other hand, described a process of tuning that is relative rather than absolute. This involved not only strings, but also (gut or string) ligatures tied round the neck. The ligature marking the place of the perfect fourth on the strings guided the player to tune the next string one "just" fourth away. Obviously the ligatures had already been placed in position by the luthier in accordance with a system of measurements.

This practice might seem in line with fretted instruments today—most obviously guitars—on which the construction includes metal bars on the neck, controlling the notes that sound when strings are played. Many scholars have translated the Persian term for hand, *dastan*, as "fret," for convenience. These frets, however, were movable, like those of the Iranian *setar*, facilitating play in different *maqams*. And it is far from certain that they were used by experienced players at all. Al Kindi described them in detail in his treatise *Risala fil luhun wan nagham*, a work intended both as an instruction book for learners and a reference book regarding oud construction principles (146, 153ff..)

The importance of establishing neck positions by tying *dastatin* (plural of *dastan*) is also clear in the *Ikhwan*:

> The length of an aliquot string is then divided into four equal sections) and the little finger fret [dastan al-khinsir] is attached at the three-quarter point towards the neck of the lute. The length of the string is then divided into nine equal parts from the top, and the first finger [sabbsba] fret is attached at the ninth nearest [the top end of] the neck of the lute; then that part of the string from the first finger fret to the bridge is divided into nine equal parts) and the ring finger [binsir] fret is attached at the ninth, its position being below the little finger fret towards the first finger fret; then that part of the string from the little finger fret to the bridge is divided into eight parts, and a further similar part is added on what remains of the string above; and it is here that the middle finger [wusta] fret is attached, its position being between the first finger and the ring finger. This is the way the lute is set up) the relationship between its strings, and the positioning of its frets. (Wright 2010, 114).

The string divisions put forward here reflect simple ratios (2:1, 3:2, 4:3, and 9:8), which indicates once again the Neoplatonic thinking of these Arab and Persian writers. We find the same positions that we find in the *Book of Melodies* of al-Ibrahim Mawsili. But al-Kindi also explained that there were multiple tuning systems in use, and that he could not cover them because they really needed to be taught by musicians. This distinction between theory and practice is yet clearer in the work of al-Farabi, a philosopher who observed that musicians could play notes *in between* the *dasatin*, as well as above and below them. It reveals the ligatures did not actually control the pitch and may have been — as indicated by both al-Urmawi and al-Ladiki—just markers (Beyhom 2020, 140). So, were they merely visual guides? And were the wound ligatures described by al-Kindi only there to aid beginners and theorists? Given that experienced players were expected to follow the voice and shift smoothly between different moods and *maqam*s, an unfretted instrument would seem more practical for them—while markers could be helpful. This seems convincing, because today we are not used to thinking about ouds as having frets at all. But given the ongoing use of movable frets in Iranian instruments, it would be a mistake to entirely rule out their uses on ouds in earlier times.

Some players were also oud makers who made their own interventions in tied ligatures. Most famous is the one purportedly introduced by the oud player al-Zalzal, midway between the second and third ligatures at the "natural" third. Al-Farabi revealed there were potentially three "anterior" ligatures between the nut and the first finger position. His work was of substantial influence on the theorist whose thinking was to dominate more than two centuries of Arab music theory, al-Urmawi, mentioned already in Chapter 9. Al-Urmawi's work launched what Arabists refer to as the "systematist" school of modal theory, bringing together an understanding of the oud and its ligatures with an attempt to capture relations between pitches and modes as a closed mathematical system. The theory was inevitably more rigid than practices of the time; it is just that the oud was the reference point for discussing theory.

Today's ouds have their four courses highest in pitch tuned in three main ways. Starting from the highest, the Arab oud descends in fourths from C to G to D to A; the Turkish descends in fourths from D to A to E to B; and the Iraqi descends in fourths from F to C to G to D. The remaining two courses (in the case of the Iraqi model there are sometimes three extra courses) may descend in fourths (popular in Turkey) or offer more harmonic support, such as G (V) and C (VI) for Arab ouds. Tuning in this way allows the two strings of lowest pitch to be used primarily as resonators and drones to support the melody. This has a long-standing tradition: Al-Kindi noted that players tended to retune the *bamm* string according to the *maqam* being played. The twentieth century yielded some further distinct tunings, as we will see later, and although the overlapping stringing seems to have been eradicated in the mainstream oud world, it is alive and well at the fringes—namely in North Africa.

11.   RECONSTRUCTIONS

As I will describe in Chapter 26, there has been a growing interest in antique instruments since at least the 1980s. Consequently, some musicians and luthiers have made replicas of these, while others have gone further back historically, building instruments for which we have no models except the images and the measurements in historical texts. The many examples of these fall into two categories. First, some aim is to create an instrument for playing, most frequently in an ensemble aiming to recapture a historical moment. And there is one, at least, where the aim was more research based, drawing on the earliest image we have for an oud in the Islamic world—the floor-painting in Qasr al-Hayr al-Gharbi of around 730 (see fig. 5).

This "research" oud was built by luthier Gerhard Söhne on the basis of studies by Eckhard Neubauer, a musicologist and scholar of the Islamic world. Söhne combined the measurements of writers discussed above, such as al-Kindi, with the image shown in figure 6 in Chapter 5 (Söhne 1994). The proportions are similar enough to be combined while making some adjustments. For instance, he took the semicircular base of the instrument as a starting point and followed the ideal proportions of al-Kindi and the *Risale*, along with al-Kindi's ideal string length and measurement for the length of the instrument. Ultimately this meant departing from the position of the bridge shown in the painting, where it is close to the base of the instrument (more like the Chinese lute called *biwa*) rather than in the widest point, as in al-Kindi. Söhne followed the *Risale* for positioning the bridge.

Of course, crucial details—not just the depth, but also the thickness of the wood, the direction of the grain, the position, and size of the braces under the face—cannot be grasped from the drawing. Söhne based his decisions about these aspects on existing instruments from the region, even while acknowledging that there could have been historical changes in the intervening centuries. For the bracing position, he drew on the description in a manuscript of ca. 1440 composed by the physician and astronomer Henri Arnaut de Zwolle, which is based on the principles of acoustics and stability. The result can be seen (but not generally heard) in the Institut für Geschichte der Arabisch-Islamischen Wissenschaften (Institute for the History of the Arab-Islamic Sciences), part of Goethe University Frankfurt, in Germany.

Another reconstruction of a historical oud has landed in a museum, but it started life as a playing instrument. This is the Persian *barbat* constructed by luthier Ibrahim Ghanbari-Mehr in Tehran in 1996. His starting point had been his observation that the Iranian oud player Mansur Nariman was playing with a raised shoulder, and that this should be avoided (Beckles Willson and Bouban 2018). He constructed an instrument inspired by a pear-shaped lute shown on the side of a silver bowl from the Sassanid era (see figure 5 in Chapter 3). It was taken up by oud player Hossein Behroozinia, who termed it *barbat* and generated some interest in it as a more authentically Persian instrument. A limited growth in *barbat* playing has paralleled the re-emergence of the oud in Iran, where it had fallen out of use and was neglected for several centuries (of this more in Chapter 30). The original instrument by Ghanbari-Mehr can be seen in the Horniman Museum and Gardens in London. Iranian luthier Mohammad Taghi Arafati also made ouds on the basis of the Sassanid illustrations.

Also in 1996, two instruments were made in Turkey by luthier Saçit Gürel, based on studies and sketches made by Fikret Karakaya, who had studied miniatures from Ottoman and Persian miniatures from the fifteenth and sixteenth centuries. One of these is the *shahrud*, the large instrument mentioned above, tuned an octave lower. These instruments, along with other historical constructions made at the same time, are what we hear in the CD recording by the Bezmara Ensemble of Istanbul called *In Search of the Lost Sound* (2000)—to which I return in Chapter 30.

Other reconstructions today tend to serve more individual interests. As we will explore in Chapter 22, during the nineteenth century, luthiers began placing labels inside their instruments, and so we can discover the genealogy of some makers and workshops. Particularly notable for the Arab world is the Damascus-based Nahhat family, while in Istanbul it is the Manol label that is most celebrated. Other luthiers have followed suit, creating their own models of ouds by famous makers such as the Nahhat family, Nazih Ghadban in Lebanon, and John Vergara in New York. Karim Othman Hassan, on the other hand, has built several ouds on the model of the Qudmany brothers of Istanbul, studying and re-making the blend of Syrian craftsmanship with Istanbul-inflected design. All these replica instruments are to be distinguished from fake historical ouds, of course, although these are in circulation as well—often patchworks of historical and contemporary fragments.

From Bezmara Ensemble's *In Search of the Lost Sound*: Arazbar Pesrev

fig.32c label from inside oud by Qudmany brothers, 1904

Fig. 32a and 32b. Oud by Selim Qudmany (1904) and reproduction by Karim Othman Hassan. Photos by Othman Hassan, reproduced with permission.

12. MORE RADICAL DESIGN EXPERIMENTS

The biggest intervention in traditional oud design happened in 1950s Iraq, a time and place of development and optimism, even a "Golden Age" of modernity and cosmopolitanism. In the new model, the strings were attached to the base of the instrument rather than to a bridge glued on the face, and they passed over an unfixed "floating" bridge like that of the violin. The result, now known as the "Iraqi oud," is something sturdier than the traditional oud, and also significantly louder in many cases. I discuss the design more fully in Chapter 25.

The increased volume of this floating-bridge oud was not sufficient to meet all the challenges of musical life in the latter half of the twentieth century. Most players today remain attached to acoustic ouds made of wood, but in order to be heard by large audiences, and among western instruments, amplification is needed. It may in some cases seem practical to use an oud with a built-in pickup, because it makes playing with a band a great deal more viable. It removes the anxiety associated with attaching microphones to delicate instruments and the potential feedback occurring when using free-standing microphones. However, adding a pickup to an existing oud means that vibrations under or on the bridge are amplified to make sound waves audible over the speaker—and this means that the air in the instrument's body, and the vibration of the oud's wooden face, are no longer relevant to the sound. When they realize this, players start to question the point of carrying around a delicate and bulky instrument and choose to make the move that guitarists made decades earlier by going fully electric.

Viken Najarian, an Armenian-American luthier in California, patented an electric oud at the turn of the twenty-first century and presented it at the Frankfurt Music Fair in 2001 (Najarian, n.d.). From the front, his E-2000 model looks very much like a traditional oud, with a spruce face and rosettes. Just the sensor strip along the bridge, and the gold volume knob give it away. But from the side, it is clearly not a traditional oud, because it is flat. More radical still is Najarian's (earlier) model E-1000, from which the face is entirely absent. Essentially this is a skeleton oud, reduced to a rim outlining the shape of the face, the neck, and an extension of the neck running under the strings and supporting the bridge. Numerous other makers make electric ouds now. One of the most refined is produced by Canadian guitar-maker Robert Godin. Called MultiOud, the shape was flat and guitar-like, but one side of the face had the oud shape, as opposed to the guitar shape. Does it sound like an oud, or like a fretless guitar? Most reviewers tend toward the latter.

A different approach to amplifying the sound of the oud is to double up the face—again following in the footsteps of guitar design. One of the earliest luthiers to take this step, and also one of the most successful, was the Turk Faruk Türünz. Two wooden faces are sandwiched together with a polymer called Nomex, which has a honeycomb-like structure. Originally used in the aviation industry, Nomex is light but very strong, and facilitates the creation of a face that is more durable (and less sensitive to humidity) than normal wooden faces. The resulting oud can be lighter and stronger, and with greater resonance; it may enhance dynamic and tonal ranges, as well as improve the instrument's sustaining power.

But do ouds ultimately *need* to be made of wood, the material from which their name originates, and to which luthiers and players attach so much importance? At the time of writing, the newest trend is in replacing the wood of the bowl with carbon fiber. Turkish luthier and engineer Emir Degirmenli has devoted several years to researching the acoustics of instruments (Degirmenli, n.d.). He makes both wooden ouds and ouds of which the body is made of carbon fiber. While Degirmenli's ouds reflect the size and shape of instruments associated now with Turkish traditions, Bashir Oud Production in Budapest, Hungary, has started making an "Iraqi" model in carbon fiber.

Part III

THE TANGLED
LIVES OF OUD PLAYERS

13. RESETTING THE STAGE

General knowledge about early oud players involves two names. The first is al-Zalzal (d. 791), associated with a particular fret, thanks to al-Farabi writing nearly a century after his death (see Chapter 10 above). The second is Ziryab (789–857), associated with a particular string (see Chapter 9 above). However, several scholars have suggested the role of Ziryab in particular needs rethinking (Davila 2009b; Reynolds 2008). Long after his death, his life was turned into a legend that bears little connection to reality. We will explore this in Chapter 16 below.

In fact, the prehistory of both al-Zalzal and Ziryab is more important for understanding early oud playing. The ancient Near East and Egypt enjoyed a musical culture that was, after all, provided predominantly by women. As was the case in Ghandara (Chapter 2), women performed in temples and they performed in courts, playing a range of instruments (drums, tambourines, plucked and bowed strings, and flutes); they also sang lamentations for rituals of mourning. Women continued to dominate the professional class of players in the first centuries of Islam, and so the earliest oud players were inevitably women.

Our sources for these oud players give us insights into the life of the Abbasid clan. Having overthrown Umayyad rule, they established the city of Baghdad as the center of the caliphate. Its elite members adopted a new lifestyle there, which was less nomadic, and they were comparatively secluded in their new palace (Moukheiber 2015). There was a lively music culture focused mainly on "gatherings" (*majalis*) for poetry and music, accompanied by food and wine (Sawa 1985; 1989; 2019).

In early Umayyad times *majalis* had been held by free women such as Sukayna bint al-Husayn and Aisha bint Talha. But in the new Baghdad court of the Abbasids, it was not free women but female courtesans (*qaynat*, "singing girls") who were central to the events. The *qaynat* belonged to a class of slaves that had access to training; they were sophisticated in their command of Arabic and accomplished in Quranic recitation in addition to poetry and songwriting. Notably, they usually played oud. All this elevated them above the slave women whose main role was to provide sexual services—*surriyya* (plural *sarari*). The *qaynat* may also have been trained in seduction and erotic practices, as being available for sexual intercourse was a part of their work. Like their accomplishment in improvising, composing, and performing poetry and song, seduction was also a means to advancement (Nielson 2012, 243–46).

It would be difficult to overestimate the number of female music-making slaves who were trained in music at the Abbasid court because no gathering or festive occasion took place without them. While public music making waxed and waned somewhat according to the caliph, there were phases in which it was part and parcel of quite breathtaking decadence that seamlessly blended food, wine, poetry, music, and probably sex. For a very intimate gathering, a single oud player would be there to accompany a singer (or a singer would play the oud to accompany herself). Oud players also performed in groups of two or three; and for large affairs they amassed in ensembles of thirty or more, all singing and playing (Sawa 1989, 150–52).

There were thousands of women who served as oud players and singers in the Abbasid times, the vast majority of whose names are lost. But some names, biographical snippets, and life fragments are preserved in surviving literature. A particularly important volume is al-Isfahani's *Kitab al-Aghani,* mentioned in Chapter 5, which compiles songs and musician-biographies according to the principles of Muslim historiography, drawing both on oral tradition and documentation. This and other shorter surviving texts allow us to explore what it meant to play an oud among the population groups most likely to play it.

Fig. 33. Cover from the Kitab al-Aghani, thirteenth-century BCE.

The most famous of the *qaynat* was Arib al-Mamuniya, who seems to have been trained by her first owner, Abdallah bin Ismail al-Marakibi, an official under the caliphate of Harun al-Rashid (Caswell 2011, 96–122). She was acquired by Caliph al-Amin (who ruled 809–813) and would eventually be freed by Caliph al-Muhtasim (who ruled 833–842). Numerous historical sources attest to her outstanding skills as a singer and composer with over a thousand songs to her name, preserved in notebooks (*dafatir*) and loose sheets (*suhuf*); they also indicate that she played and taught oud, while being a poet who was skilled in calligraphy along with popular games backgammon and chess. Another reason multiple sources refer to her is that she earned so much money that she was able to retire from the court, set up her own home, and employ and train numerous slaves of her own (Moukheiber 2015, 132ff.).

The level of self-advancement that Arib attained was rare, but she was not the only one to find upward mobility. The most beautiful, skilled, sharp-witted, and courageous *qaynat* could get themselves traded between wealthy men or get themselves profitably hired in taverns and private homes. They could also try to arrange their legal status to their advantage: some had contracts that freed them from their owners upon the birth of a child (a process that earned them the title *umm walad*

"mother of a child"); others managed to negotiate or buy their freedom. These rights were not available to slaves in the ancient world and contemporary West.

Nevertheless, Arib's case also emphasizes both the structural, institutional strength of the patriarchy and the fact that women had no rights to exercise their own sexual choices. When Arib returned to a lover she had prior to being owned by al-Marakibi, al-Marakibi pursued them and imprisoned the lover. Arib sought help from Caliph Mamun, who appointed a judge in Islamic law (*qadi*) to decide on her ownership. Mamun, however, also wanted Arib, and finding that the judge's verdict did not help, he appointed a further judge and then bought her for himself (Stigelbauer 1975, 21–27). In other words, four elite men negotiated the sexual activities of this oud-playing woman between them. Women did not have such authority, and it seems from other stories that Arib's primary technique of making her case was dramatic but also legalistic self-presentation. Following her beating by al-Marakibi, for example, she challenged his right to inflict such harm and demanded that she be recognized as free or sold to another master; when the lover himself was arrested and whipped, she rode a mule to the prison, removed her veil, and proclaimed again that either she was free or that she should be sold to another owner (Gordon 2017, 29).

Understanding the actions of women such as Arib is far from straightforward, because they lived in a time of intense male anxiety about religious and social change. Quite apart from the fact that the society was still elaborating what Islam meant, religious scholars began to be concerned about the decadence of the caliphate, and there was an emerging sense of a need to consolidate an ethical code for men's behavior. The scholars challenged what they saw as the impropriety of the ruling elite. Rulers were supposed to exemplify Islamic modesty and restraint, rather than display a life of flamboyant entertainment. Legal, literary, and historical discussions proliferated, intended to regulate worldly pleasures, and *qaynat* such as Arib became rhetorical figures in the ensuing discourse. Writers who described *qaynat* disapprovingly, or described their own or someone's resistance to the charms of *qaynat*, were ultimately articulating their own piousness (Moukheiber 2015, 31–34).

A central problem was the close association between listening to music and drinking wine, and the state of *tarab* (ecstasy) that segued smoothly into sexual activity. Arabic poetry, both pre-Islamic and of the Islamic era, celebrates, rather than despises, this connection. But more censorious texts of the time identified the dangers that *qaynat* embodied for men—and thus for proper society. Al-Jahiz's *The Epistle of the Singing Girls* observed that *qaynat* led traders and patrons into bankruptcy, debt, and debauchery, neglect of their family and loss of their social standing. Similarly recognizing that this problem was primarily that of such elite men, another commentator, Ibn al-Washa, nevertheless identified the *qaynat* as inherently corrupting society as well (Nielson 2012, 251ff.). This aggressively misogynist thread would continue for centuries, and can be traced even in the apparently innocuous or celebratory references to women in poetry. If women were truly able to render men speechless by outshining the moon, as some noted, of course they were an enormous threat to the male establishment as well (Prince-Eichner 2016, 76).

Fig. 34. Tavern scene. Codex A.F. 9 folio 42 verso. Austrian National Library. Cod. A.F.9, fol.42v: Makamen.

14.   MEET ARIB, SHARIYA, AND ULAYYA

By the tenth century, the pietist movement had become so strong that it was used to legitimize home raids and arrests of women. Religious scholar Ibn Abi al-Dunya (d. 894) published a monograph about the dangers of music's emotional impact, *Dhamm al-malahi* (*Tracts on Listening to Music*). He was not only critical of the *qaynat*; he also asserted that musical instruments were vehicles for entertainment and therefore diversions from the correct moral path (Shiloah 1995, 63–64). Al-Dunya's highly influential text contributed to burgeoning discussions about which types of music could be listened to, and where, when, and how they could be performed. This context is one in which we find our most important source, al-Isfahani's *Book of Songs*. Al-Isfahani seems to have attempted to respond to the ongoing debate by identifying all the positive values that music making had brought the Islamic empire in the first centuries of its existence (Nielson 2012, 259).

As traced in a range of sources, Arib's own biography suggests how she worked effectively within the ethical code even after having extracted herself from performing duties of all kinds. According to the memoirs of the *qadi* al-Muhaassin, after her retirement she visited a wealthy admirer from her past, Ibrahim al-Mudabbir, who had since amassed a great fortune (Margoliouth 1922, 144–46). She claimed to have longed for him, and she brought with her an entourage of musicians who sang for them both, and even sang a poem composed by al-Mudabbir, to the melody and in the style instructed by Arib. He rewarded her musicians with gifts worth 1,000 dinars, and they sat together until sunset. Just before she left, Arib put her primary request to him: she wished to buy an estate from his wife. Only once this purchase had been secured did she leave.

This story also contains an anecdote in which al-Mudabbir asks Arib herself to sing his poem and she reproaches him, as they both know that she has "repented" her former life as a *qayna*. By passing the task to her own slaves and instructing them, though music, how to flatter al-Mudabbir, she was able to make the property deal she sought without compromising her propriety. In this story, she used her musical skills to advance herself, but she transferred the risk of actual performance to other women.

Unlike the majority of Abbasid slaves, who were brought from afar by traders, *qaynat* were frequently native born (even if to newly arrived enslaved mothers), probably because a mother tongue in Arabic was the best starting point for the sharp wit they needed in performance poetry. Nevertheless, they were subjects of male commodification, just as were the less elevated concubines, and honed their skills to meet the demands of the patriarchy.

THE TANGLED LIVES OF OUD PLAYERS

Arib's rival at court, Shariya, provides a good example, as a younger woman born in Basra who had been purchased by the Abbasid prince Ibrahim al-Mahdi. As she rose to prominence as a singer, she was mocked for not playing the oud, and subsequently added this skill to her portfolio to keep up (Moukheiber 2019, 174–75). Al-Isfahani emphasized how listeners were stunned by her rare musical skill and recognized her high artistry. Their style of appreciation, carefully termed *ajab* by al-Isfahani, was distinct from the more dangerous emotional state of *tarab* most often associated with musical pleasure (Moukheiber 2019, 175–76). He observed that Shariya's skill and training made her a lucrative investment for elite traders; having been bought by al Mahdi for no more than 300 dinars, after a year's further voice training, the musician al-Mawsili (who had himself declined to buy her when al-Mahdi bought her) offered 3,000 dinars for her purchase (Stigelbauer 1975, 42).

Because all the contemporary discussions about music were essentially about men, and the dangers of men submitting themselves to the emotional effect of music, women who were not enslaved fared little better as musicians. Ultimately the legal distinction between "free" and "enslaved" musicians was based on the status of the man who acknowledged (or claimed) he had fathered her child(ren). Once again, male honor was the deciding factor in any circumstance.

For example, Ulayya (d. 825) was born to a female slave, but her father was the third Abbasid caliph, al-Mansur (who ruled 775–85)—and this set her fortunes apart from those of Arib and Shariya. However, free female musicians such as Ulayya may have stirred up even greater anxiety, and the men wishing to enjoy or share their musical activity had to be all the more circumspect about how they did so. The fact that Ulayya was a composer and musician was a matter of shame for her half-brother—and future caliph—Harun al-Rashid when he first discovered it, and it was subsequently an only half-open secret at court. When her songs were performed by slaves in *majalis*, her authorship was not to be mentioned, for this cast a shadow on her (and, by extension, the men associated with her).

One of al-Isfahani's anecdotes describes the caliph's way of presenting her to a courtier, which involved leading him to a pavilion and a series of locked doors (Moukheiber 2019, 169ff.). The caliph locked each one behind them as they proceeded, while knocking to send a message forward that he wished to hear oud and singing. Al-Isfahani describes how restrained the caliph and his courtier were able to be in their enjoyment—responding to the music and feeling the appropriate *tarab* (ecstasy) but controlling their behaviors appropriately: the caliph did a solitary dance, and the courtier beat his head against the wall.

Ulayya was certainly materially privileged, but she must have felt entirely dependent on her brother the caliph for authorization when it came to music making. When he died, she seems to have been too terrified to sing until the next caliph, her brother's successor, invited her to do so. The "free" oud player in this case was socially and professionally constrained and living in precariousness because she had developed her artistic interests and talents. The case of a *qayna* called Inan was very similar; when the master of this outstanding poetess died, she was sold at a regular slave market and her career ended.

These fragments of biography are striking today even in the early twenty-first century, in which it is comparatively rare for women to play the oud, and the anxiety and shame associated with them doing so remains in some quarters. We will revisit this topic in Chapters 32 and 40.

Fig. 35. Vintage postcard. Origin, date and copyright untraced.

15.   FIELD BATTLES

Life in Abbasid times was precarious in many spheres of life (including that of the ruling classes), and musicians did not escape the dramatic changes of fortune that could occur from one day to the next. The favor of a patron could enhance or even secure the livelihood of a musician, while disfavor brought widespread disparagement and potentially existential threat.

Sometimes it was singing competitions that provided the stage for momentous judgments, such as the famous one that took place late in the lives of Arib and Shariya. Neither of them was singing any longer, but each had their own trained choir of singers (Imhof 2013, 4ff.), and Caliph al-Mutawakkil invited them to compete, along with their slave singers. The audience was divided by support for one or the other camp, and Shariya made a fatal error, claiming authorship of a song that was not her own. Arib humiliated her ruthlessly by calling for a singer named Athath to be brought and asking him to sing a particular song by one al-Zubayr ibn Dahman. This turned out to be the same song. Shariya's dishonesty lost her the competition and brought herself into disgrace (Gordon 2004, 70–73).

Arib is reported to have commanded her team of women to sing that night by saying, "Take the way of truth and steer us clear of falsehood. Sing in the ancient way!" Her expression was not only chiding of Shariya, but also was a way of positioning herself on one side of a poetic and musical culture that was divided by competing attitudes to tradition and innovation (Gordon 2004, 73; Imhof 2013). While the younger Shariya was associated with new trends brought from Persia, Arib was an upholder of repertoires and traditions associated by then with the Arabs. Their preferences were partly shaped by age, but also by leading male musicians, who bought and sold them as slaves, and also taught some of them. Shariya was a pupil of the musician most associated with the progressive trends, Ishaq al-Mahdi, who challenged the more traditional attitude of the equally celebrated Ibrahim al-Mawsili.

These men came to prominence as performers thanks to influence from abroad (most obviously Persia), an influence that led to the role of professional music making previously occupied by women alone being taken up by men. By the ninth century, the oud was effectively gender-neutral. Both al-Mahdi and al-Mawsili accompanied themselves on the oud while singing, even while neither seems to have been outstanding on the instrument, and like many singers, preferred to have a dedicated oud player support them in performance (Sawa 1989, 150).

At the heart of the music culture, after all, was poetry, and—as an extension to that—song. The oud had a predominantly supporting role, just as did the tanbur (long-necked lute), so that moments of glory were largely constrained to preludes to songs, melodic responses to a singer's phrases, or interludes and postludes. Nevertheless, sometimes players had to entertain the caliph by competing against one another as soloists. Caliph al-Wathiq, himself a singer and an oud player, demanded that oud players al-Zalzal and Mulahiz should each perform at his *majlis* so that the best player could be identified (Sawa 1989, 153).

Other competitions were more obviously bound up with economics and took place on the slave market itself. There were battles over the sales of *qaynat* because talented slaves (both male and female) were a form of cultural capital, elevating the status of their owners. When al-Mawsili offered 3,000 dinars for Shariya, the sale did not go through because the woman who had previously sold her to al-Mahdi (a woman who may or may not have been her mother), attempted to block it by appealing to the caliph. Al-Mawsili nevertheless heard about what she was doing and intervened first, claiming that he had married her. The falsity of this claim emerged only after some years (during which Caliph al-Muhtasim made a vain attempt to buy her for no less than 70,000 dinars), on the death of

al-Mawsili. Nevertheless, al-Mawsili's heiress Maimuna was able to sell her to Caliph al-Muhtasim, albeit for the relatively modest sum of 5,500 dinars (Stigelbauer 1975, 42).

Fig. 36. Detail showing musicians on a vessel, the Blacas Ewer, Mosul. British Museum.

Other battles over women were less about male possession of cultural capital than the more basic male money-making. Al-Mawsili was reputedly the first of the music educators to train "beautiful" women—a term interpreted today by some to mean light-skinned, probably European or Armenian (Gordon 2017, 33–34). Whether or not it was really him alone who brought about the change, it seems that light-skinned women were valued for their looks alone, whereas women with darker skin needed extra qualities—such as being able to sing and play instruments—in order to move beyond menial domestic duties. According to his son, al-Mawsili avoided Chinese, Indians, Sindhis, and Africans, buying only light-skinned women to train as *qaynat* (Caswell 2011, 13–17, 221–22).

Skin color was a concern for one of the most mythologized oud-playing singers of the era, the dark-skinned Ziryab, mentioned at the start of this section. A highly paid, Baghdad-trained musician (probably a slave, although the biographies are not entirely clear), Ziryab left the capital in 813 after Caliph al-Amin was deposed and killed. The subsequent Caliph al-Mamun, having attacked al-Amin's decadent lifestyle, issued a moratorium on music at court (even while he partook of music and wine in private), so Ziryab may have been a victim of this cultural-political switch. Ziryab passed

through Syria before living in Tunisia under the Aghlabid emir Ziyadat Allah I, until he angered the emir and was banished (Davila 2009b, 128). He arrived in Cordoba in 822. His dark skin led him to be the target of both racist and sexual jokes (Reynolds 2008, 156), but his work at the Umayyad court in Cordoba was evidently substantial.

This Umayyad court, an empire-in-exile, saw three main phases in its courtly music making. In the first phase, which probably only got started in the reign of al-Hakam I (who ruled 796–822), the female musicians were trained in Medina and Baghdad, and the resulting music culture was likely very similar to the ones in those Eastern centers of Islam (Reynolds 2017). Subsequently, training took place in Cordoba itself, which fostered the development of new branches of repertoire and stylistic development, even while this was based on and perhaps combined the two foundational (and rival) styles of Medina and Baghdad. After the Berber defeat of Cordoba in 1013 and the fragmentation of the Umayyad reign into rival principalities, musical training took place primarily in Seville. By this time, the styles associated with Cordoba were being increasingly transformed by local influences, including songs of Christians. It was also the time in which the new regional repertoires such as the genres of *muwashshah* and *zajal* spread more extensively, through the movements of *qaynat* throughout the Arabic-speaking North Africa and Near East.

No direct comparison is possible between the lives of *qaynat* at the Abbasid court in Baghdad and those who lived at the time of the Umayyads in Cordoba, because the men writing texts about the latter had very different preoccupations and altogether much less anxiety about sexuality. The *qaynat* appear primarily as projections of the caliphs' desires, as if they were magical music-therapists whose songs were a balm for their anxious hearts, solace in moments of sadness, and a sedative in times of insomnia. They were also good company.

Nevertheless one distinct element in their writings suggests a clear distinction from Baghdad; *qaynat* living in both Cordoba and Seville benefitted even more from educational opportunities than did those in Baghdad, which allowed them to become learned in fields that had previously been the domain of men, such as logic, philosophy, geometry, astronomy, astrology, and even fencing. They were thus equipped to offer even more (above their physical appeal, poetry, song, and oud playing) than the *qaynat* of Baghdad, where it seems additional tasks had more to do with being a maid, preparing garments, and occasionally accompanying their owners on walks (Reynolds 2017).

The case of Ziryab's role in Cordoba is interesting because while his difficult temperament, frivolity, and frequently undignified behavior is clear from all contemporary reports from the people who knew him, two highly selective, much later textual sources came to dominate how he was understood (Davila 2009b; Reynolds 2008). One of these was written by a probable family descendent, Aslam ibn Abd al-Aziz, who celebrates Ziryab as outshining all other singers and as an outstanding model of courtly behavior. He claims that Ziryab revolutionized Cordoban aesthetics with his introduction of a new hairstyle, deodorant, drinking glasses (rather than metal cups), color changes in seasonal clothing, and extensive recipes. Abd al-Aziz's account shaped the other sources, including a biographical account of Ziryab written in seventeenth-century Cairo by Shihab al-Dın Ahmad al-Maqqari (d. 1632). This was altogether more extreme and hagiographical, claiming that Ziryab shaped Andalusian culture in unprecedented ways and wielded more influence than has ever been attributed to a musician in Arab Islamic culture.

Abd al-Aziz probably wrote *Akhbar Ziryab* in the first half of the eleventh century, and according to Dwight Reynolds (2008), it was likely an expression of a family desire for Umayyad revival, following its collapse and fragmentation. But what about al-Maqqari? Why did he extract and amplify the positive accounts of Ziryab so systematically from the very mixed historical sources he used? Was there already a noble legend that he chose to protect? Or did he falsify the historical record in order to create a new one? The answer may lie in the series of biographical studies in which his account was published. Shaped by the ongoing inter-clan rivalry between Umayyad and Abbasids that had led to the original exiling of the Umayyads and their capital in exile in Spain, this was intended to demonstrate the historical superiority of al-Andalus. Through al-Maqqari's writing, the singer and oud player Ziryab became a rhetorical figure through whom the lost golden age of al-Andalus could exist—if only as a realm of nostalgia and desire (Reynolds 2008, 166).

This mythologization of Ziryab haunts narratives about oud players even today. As we will see in Chapter 39, for example, Ziryab was a useful rhetorical figure through which to glorify the Iraqi oud player Munir Bashir when he made his celebrated concert appearances in France and Switzerland in the early 1970s. The intense rivalry that has shaped the posthumous existence of Ziryab has continued to shape oud traditions as well. In particular there are other Iraqi musicians whose public personas are shaped by intense competitiveness: Jamil Bashir and Munir Bashir with their forcefully soloistic attitudes (Chapters 31 and 38), and Naseer Shamma, who has identified himself as heir to Ziryab, magically erasing the intervening centuries and players.

Fig 37. A famous image associated with the mythologised Ziryab, used here on an Iraqi postage stamp.

16.   MUSICAL INTERACTIONS BETWEEN WOMEN AND MEN

If we glanced through historical literature, which is shaped so strongly by anxiety about male propriety, we might imagine that that the only musical relations between women and men played out around overtly sexualized interaction. However, when we read the literature more closely, we discover two less fraught observations. One of these relates to the wit of women. Their repartee and improvised poetry was part and parcel of their public role as performers, and they frequently outshone the men they entertained, and with whom they competed (of this more below). The other observation granted them less limelight; they were supposed to be the voice boxes of male composers. Ziryab either owned or trained thirty-eight female slaves under Caliph al-Rahman II, and they secured his income and his legacy because he was rewarded for their performances of his music. According to one account, they were not only performers but actually contributed to his song-writing process. His slaves Ghizalan and Hunayda used their ouds to help him consolidate the melodies that came to his mind at night, and then played them to him when asked the next day. He would build further on the melodies, also using his own oud. These two slaves were known as "Ziryab's two (song) holders"(*masikatayn*). They were essentially the invisible facilitators of his work (Davila 2009b, 130,134). Another of his slaves, named Shanif (Delightful), was

understood as the authentic source for his songs after his death, and likely had a role in their creation.

Beyond these examples, the most interesting source for exploring interactions between women and men is the fictional *1001 Nights*. Notwithstanding the fantastical elaborations of the storytelling genre, the *1001 Nights* allows us to further flesh out what we can glean from the other more strictly historical sources. Many stories of the *Nights* are based on happenings in Baghdad in Abbasid times, and they help us imagine richer ways in which the oud could be a vehicle in both the competitive and the sexualized strands of music making—in fact, how they could be entangled.

Some of these reinforce the patriarchy of the time. For example, one story involves the musician and slave trader Ibrahim al-Mahdi, who is entranced by the glimpse of a wrist and hand through a window as he passes the house of a merchant. He manages to infiltrate the house (pretending to be in the company of some distinguished visitors) and is entertained with food and wine, and then a *qayna*. Although moved by her performance, he identifies a fault in it, to which she responds with anger. He asks for an oud to demonstrate what he means, and astonishes everyone present with his prowess. His performance, along with his family status as uncle of the caliph, which until that moment he had hidden, is sufficient for him to be offered sight of all the female wrists and hands in the house. When he finds the one he is looking for, which belongs to the merchant's sister, the merchant is so honored by the royalty in his house that he immediately "gives" his sister to him, along with a bag of gold (Lyons and Lyons 2010b, 110ff.).

Nevertheless, other stories are more suggestive of the strengths of women. One is an immensely protracted tale that is framed by the conflict between Byzantium and Caesarea, and a petition to the powerful ruler Omar that he come to the aid of Byzantium (Istanbul). The son of Omar, Sharkan, leads forth an army but strays into the hands of the Princess Abriza, daughter of the king of Rum. Abriza turns out to be physically and intellectually a challenge to Sharkan and disarms him in all ways: with her physical fighting, with her cunning, and later with wine, playing the oud (among other instruments), and singing in Arabic (Lyons and Lyons 2010a, 322ff.).

Yet more striking is a story that reveals a style of female solidarity, "The Story of the Porter and the Three Ladies," set in Baghdad during one of the caliphates (Lyons and Lyons 2010a, 50ff.). Three women have received a motley group of visitors to their home. There is a porter who helped carry food from the market, the caliph, his vizier, and his executioner (the latter three are incognito), and three one-eyed dervishes. All the guests are in the women's home on one condition, namely that they are not to concern themselves with matters that are not their business. The party is extravagant, and at first intensely pleasurable (lavish food and drink, entertainment by passing musicians, erotic games in a sunken pool), but it comes to involve some ritualistic whipping and then comforting of female dogs. This upsets the guests, who are further upset later when one of the women plays the oud and sings, because the music prompts another of the women to cry out and tear her dress open from top to toe. The guests find themselves gaping at a naked body covered in welts and bruises. They watch her put on a fresh dress, but when the oud-playing starts up again she repeats her cry, tearing and stripping. The guests are appalled, and after the third time, despite the injunction, they persuade the porter to pose the question they all need answered. What is the meaning of this terrible cruelty and suffering in this magnificent home?

The home of the women, we realize, while initially seeming merely a space of sensual pleasures, comes gradually to be revealed to be a site for the reliving of horrific violence. In it, the role of the oud is to force engagement with the scars on body and psyche left by her marriage. The ensemble of player and oud is powerful in shifting the attention of listening guests because they have been captivated by the woman as an object of desire. They find themselves exposed to her wounds and her treatment as a piece of domestic sexual property, and they become part of her repetitively experienced pain.

The women's response is to tell them that they have broken their agreement to not ask questions, and prepare to have them tied up to be killed. But before completing this project, the women invite the men to tell their stories. In the way of the *1001 Nights*, the guests' stories branch into other stories, and in due course everyone learns the truth in the body of the woman who stripped. Her welts are the marks of her husband's thrashing, which he inflicted in his rage upon feeling that his honor was besmirched after she had been assaulted in the market. As the story continues, all the women's sufferings are revealed, along with those of the female dogs, who turn out to have originally been sisters of the first of the three women. They are able to return to their human form thanks to the timely intervention of a she-devil.

Given the style of the *1001 Nights,* it is unsurprising that the ultimate ending is conventional. The caliph sees that wrongs are avenged, and he arranges new marriages between the women and the one-eyed dervishes (who turn out to have originally been kings, and he appoints them as chamberlains in his court); and the cycle of normative homemaking can begin again (potentially with all its violence). But the story exemplifies how the thought and expressiveness of women may be important socially and politically.

Understanding that the oud can have this role connects us with its memorial role today. I mentioned Shamma's *Happened in al-Amiriya* in the introduction, but another example is worth mentioning. One of the memorial events held after the tragic fire at London's Grenfell Tower in June 2017, in which more than seventy people lost their lives, was a service of remembrance in St. Paul's Cathedral. It included musical performances chosen in collaboration with survivors, and one of these was played on the oud by Syrian musician Rihab Azar (Beckles Willson 2019b, 459—60, 477). The creative impulse—Azar's own gently reflective composition for the event—was in stark contrast to the corporate greed that allowed the Grenfell disaster to take place. Surely it allowed listeners a moment to hope and strive for a better world.

Part IV:

BRIDGES TO AND FROM EUROPE

17. WHAT IS THE EUROPEAN LUTE?

The instrument we know as the lute today is most probably descended from the ouds played at the Umayyad court, and more generally the instruments played by Arabs living in the South of Europe from the ninth to the thirteenth century. Just the oud's name changed; as it moved northward the Spanish *laud* became the French *luth*, and the German *Laute*, the Italian *lauto* or *liuto*, and the Flemish *luit*. *Luit* also meant vagina (Craig-McFeely 2002, 30), and this coincidence must have affected the significance of the oud in the Netherlands region and beyond, which we will explore further below. Meanwhile, the construction remained constant for some centuries, according to the images that survive. Five courses of strings remained typical, as did the semi-spherical area at the base of the bowl.

The lives of the oud and the lute (*laud, luth, lauto...*) subsequently developed in parallel, and were probably connected despite physical distance. Geometry remained important, most obviously in rosette designs. Even while Europeans introduced new floral designs to rosettes over time, the divisions and proportions of decorations remained geometric, in line with their interests in the connections between proportion, symbolism, and the planets (Lundberg 1992, 227). These same interests extended the tradition of theoretical borrowing that connected Plato,

Pythagoras, and al-Kindi, impacting the ideas about lute proportions. As we saw in Chapter 7, Arab writers such as al-Kindi had argued that pitch ratios Pythagoras had identified in string resonances would affect the Platonic "microcosm" of the human being. In Europe, Boethius (480–524 CE) built on Plato to establish three categories: *musica mundana* (music of the spheres), *musica humana* (ruling that the proportions of harmony controlling the universe also control humanity), and *musica instrumentalis* (audible, human-made music). When lutes were constructed with Pythagorean ratios, they were in tune with the universe. As they were constructed increasingly in a range of sizes, the ratios shaped the relations between instruments as well; lutes that were pitched one octave apart had a size ratio of 1:2, the descant lute had a string length of two-thirds that of the alto (2:3), and so on (Lundberg 1992, 216–27, 222–23).

Along with this very deep historical bond between oud and lute, there were changes that happened to each of them more or less simultaneously. The new sixth course of strings can be traced first on a European lute in 1470 and was widespread by 1500. Al-Ladiqi's writing on Egypt at around the same time mentions an oud with a sixth string—the *oud akmal* (Neubauer 1993, 308). This kind of parallel development could have been a result of movement in and out of urban and court centers by musicians, craftsman, diplomats, and writers. The French writer Seigneur de Villamont wrote about the oud players of Cairo, where he spent some months during the years 1589–1590. He noted the color of the strings were white, yellow, blue, green, and red, and wrote that they could just as well be used for lutes of Venice and Padua, although they were less harmonious as all were wound, rather like the bass strings of European instruments. He wrote that most of the "Greek," "Turkish," and "Moorish" residents picked up their oud to play as a daily habit, bringing great pleasure to others. Good players were regarded as excellent people (Neubauer 1993, 313; Villamont 2012 [1595]).

The French traveler, scientist, and diplomat Pierre Belon (1517–1564) published similar findings from his visit to Istanbul in 1574. He observed very widespread oud playing (more widespread than the lute in Europe, he said) and described string making. The strings were colored red, blue, green, yellow, and white, and although they had a less harmonious sound, they could be used on European lutes (Neubauer 1993, 313). In fact, the string color was a quality that had long been absorbed deeply into European thinking. Already in the tenth century, on the novel staff notation for music associated with Guido di Arezzo (d. 1050), the two most important lines were red (for C) and yellow (for F). Guido noted that the lines were "imitations of strings"—and they seem to refer to the *mathna* and *zir*.

The earliest account of the structure of the European lute is by physician, astrologer, and astronomer Henri Arnault de Zwolle. He seems to indicate that in broad terms, the oud proportions were intact at the time he was writing (ca. 1440), with the semicircular cross section at the widest point of the body (Van Edwards 2011). That said, his diagram is idiosyncratic, with a strangely rounded face contour attached to an oddly long neck, while paintings of the time are more like the oud. However, in this period, a change in playing styles was underway, and this would eventually divide the oud from the lute quite distinctly. In 1487, Flemish theorist and composer Johannes de Tinctoris wrote that players had begun transferring several musical lines—hitherto played by a group of three or four lutenists—onto one instrument. This type of complexity would have been extremely difficult with a pick. It must have led players increasingly to drop it and use their fingers as they developed their activities as soloists (Lundberg 1992, 212–14).

A new model of lute seems to have emerged just a little later in Italy, where numerous German luthiers settled during the 1500s. Some fled their homes in the German Peasants' War (1524–1525) and Schmalkaldic War (1546–1547), others were simply attracted by the wealth of the region and the availability of imported woods arriving in Venice. The new body shape was relatively elongated, made of nine or eleven ribs in harder materials—ivory, whalebone, ebony, and rosewood, probably ash and maple as well. The semicircular cross section of the oud had disappeared; the base was slightly flattened. The earliest surviving lute has the new narrow form (it was made by Laux Maler, a German in Bologna 1485–1552), as does a surviving instrument by his contemporary there Hans Frei. This shape dominated the Renaissance period, although lutes made in Venice by the celebrated Tieffenbrucker family of luthiers were slightly broader (Hellwig 1974, 22–23).

If the history of the oud and the lute seem to diverge at this point, it is worth noting that there were lutes made in Venice in the 1630s onward that had more rounded bodies. The associated makers were the Sellas family, Pietro and Giovanni Railich, and Christofolo Koch. Whereas the long European lute of the time had a ratio of 1:0.6 for the length to width of the body, the new rounded ones were nearer to 1:0.9. Some scholars have suggested they represent a glance backward (Hellwig 1974, 23–24). But given the position of Venice on the Silk Road, they are perhaps just as likely to have resulted from the ongoing influence of the Arab world. Certainly the rare woods and ivory used by luthiers in Venice could be evidence of the raw materials entering the port from the East.

Fig. 38. Lute. Attributed to Wendelin Tieffenbrucker (late 16th century). The Metropolitan Museum of Art, public domain.

18.   MEET ELISABETTA, PAOLA, IRENE AND MARY

Another very interesting point of comparison between European and Middle Eastern ouds is the way they served as vehicles for women to earn their keep. Women were at relative liberty in Italian society until around 1350, but from then on there were increasing constraints on their activities. Men gradually took over the public space, restricting women to unpaid labor in domestic environments and denying them professional opportunities. Any creative activity was frowned upon, understood as a frivolous distraction from their main role, which was looking after the household and the family (H. M. Brown 1986, 79). By the fifteenth century the only profession available to women was procuring, and the lute was one of the tools of this trade.

Thus when the English traveler and writer Thomas Coryat (ca. 1577–1617) published a two-volume account of the five-month walk he took through France, Italy, Switzerland, Germany, and the Netherlands in 1608 (*Coryats Crudities: Hastily gobbled up in Five Moneth's Travels*, 1611), his account of Venice referred extensively to courtesans. A courtesan will, he claimed, "endeavour to enchant thee, partly with her melodious notes that she warbles out upon her lute" (Coryat 1905, 1:405). He also noted that the wives of gentlemen were hidden away from public spaces unless there were major events to attend (when they could be present only when veiled).

The earliest courtesan whom we can trace with any clarity is Elisabetta Condulmer, who was born in Venice in the 1490s. Among the possessions she left on her death were four lutes, and her home was set up with plentiful chairs to accommodate an audience for concerts, and lavishly furnished and hung with contemporary paintings (sacred and profane). We saw in Chapter 14 that family honor was a deciding factor for women under the Abbasids of Baghdad, and it seems that in Venice, the lives of women were similarly dictated by their family status.

Condulmer's life as a procuress was probably a function of her mother's doubtful status, as well as the rather modest legacy bequeathed by her nobleman father. But she made the best of the cards she was dealt in life, managing to secure the family house—buying out her brothers' shares, presumably through her courtesan earnings—as well as securing herself a husband. It is likely that her marriage to Gabriel di Angeli was a convenience enabling her to avoid certain restrictive legislations. On her death, she had seven children from three other men, and left them the bulk of her legacy (P. F. Brown 2004, 173–81).

Paola Provesin was one of the last courtesans of Venice, and she died in 1638. Her apartment on Piazza San Marco had been rented for her by a noble patron, Tommaso Contarini, who had also funded her training in music, painting, and poetry. It was lavishly decorated with paintings, damask, and leather furnishings. It also contained a mass of musical scores and an array of musical instruments, including two lutes (one ivory) and six theorboes, along with two keyboard instruments—a spinet and a harpsichord. Paola lived at a time when women had once again regained some professional opportunities and had become major forces in the music life of Italy more broadly. She left all her worldly possessions to charity (P. F. Brown 2012, 24).

From these biographies we can see that the courtesans of Venice were an educated class of woman among a broader class of women employed for sexual favors—not unlike the *qaynat*. However, social attitudes were arguably more ambiguous when it came to music. On the one hand, music was understood as a danger, particularly when the lute was involved. Women who played music were viewed with disapproval, and if men discussed them, they had to do so with care, so as not to besmirch their own reputations. Christian doctrine cast prostitution as a sin. However, the priesthood was tolerant (even beneficent), so courtesans were welcomed in the churches. Perhaps most fundamentally, courtesans were taxpayers, and important to the city's economy, so they had to be accommodated rather than outlawed. European society more broadly cultivated a highly ambiguous relationship with music and morality. This was distinct from the mainstream Islamic cultures of the time. In short, even while music was understood as profane in many contexts, it was also celebrated as a means to spiritual elevation. Renaissance humanists invoked the Platonic harmony of the spheres (discussed in Chapter 17) to write about the beauty of instruments and their sounds. Music, they argued, was not only of the flesh; it connected humanity with nature, earth with heavens. This kind of argument meant that some upper-class women were allowed to play music domestically, even if not for financial reward. From the age of three, the commoner orphan Irene di Spilimbergo was brought up by her maternal grandfather, Zuan Paolo da Ponte, who enabled her to study painting with Titian and music with lutenist Bartolomeo Gazza and composer Ippolito Tromboncino. Her biographer observed that while Irene was extremely ambitious and competitive about her skills, she always behaved decorously, as a gentlewoman (P. F. Brown 2012, 22).

Fig. 39. A courtesan with a lute (oil on canvas) by Jan Gerritsz van Bronckhorst (c. 1603–1661).

BRIDGES TO AND FROM EUROPE

Ultimately it is likely that the glamorous homes in which courtesans welcomed their clients were very similar to those of noblewomen, and as the Umayyad rule fragmented in Southern Spain, and *qaynat* were sold to Christian noblemen, there may have been a blurring of categories. Presumably while these noblemen enjoyed music making in their homes, they also enjoyed the long tradition of musical seduction of which the *qaynat* were part. Further north, the Flemish school of painting seems to have drawn heavily on the fact that the Flemish word *luit* meant not only lute, but also vagina (Craig-McFeely 2002, 301). Hundreds of paintings by artists such as Johannes, Vermeer, Dirck van Baburen, and Jan Sten incorporate the lute in order to eroticize a scene, whether it appears in the arms of a procuress, hung on a wall, or played by a rogueish-looking man.

And yet the lute also appears in illustrations of the Cantigas de Santa Maria, a celebration of the miracles of the Virgin Mary, and in numerous paintings from the Italian Renaissance we see lutes in the arms of angels. These depictions may have been intended to "rescue" the reputations of men who enjoyed music of the lute. Saint Cecilia—patron saint of music—is portrayed in Riccardo Quartararo's painting of 1490 holding a palm frond and the Gospels, while a lute-playing angel kneels at her feet.

Some of the more subtle ambiguities of the lute in Europe emerge in a popular genre of French poetry from the 1540s and 1550s, in which it appears as a companion and muse, more often than not anthropomorphized. Sometimes the rounded belly of the lute symbolizes fertility and voluptuousness, and sometimes the neck was phallic (a tendency very clear in Caravaggio's painting *The Musicians*), while both male and female poets often cultivated ambiguity in its gender.

Fig. 40. Lute. Sixtus Rauchwolff, 1596. The Metropolitan Museum of Art, public domain.

Some of the more striking poems by women, nonetheless, present the lute as if it were a male companion with desires at odds with their own. In one daring riddle poem of the 1570s (attributed to Madeleine de l'Aubespine or Héliette de Vivonne) the subject takes the "neck," "touching and working it, so that it will be in a state to give me pleasure" (Zecher 2000, 787–88). As the poem goes on, the subject throws herself on the bed and, "moving forcefully... among a thousand sweetnesses," achieves her desire. If it slackens, she straightens it with her hand...

In England, the lute's golden age happened later than on the European continent, lasting from around 1570 until it waned in 1630. The anthropomorphic, muse-like quality of the instrument was equally important in England, but it developed a different significance. The association with fertility was intact, particularly in the visual dimension. But the dimension of sound was more explicitly idealized as a realm in which complex and otherwise inarticulable feelings could be expressed in harmony (Craig-McFeely 2002, 300). One logical outcome of this was that it could be claimed to convey a woman's sophistication and strength, and we can trace this in portraits of noble poets Lady Mary Wroth and Lady Anne Clifford. Another result was that it advertised a woman's suitability not just for sex but for marriage. Mary Burwell's *Lute Tutor* (ca. 1660–1672)

focuses explicitly on the latter, effectively taming and domesticating the seductive potential of a woman with an oud, while giving it a wholly positive spin:

The beauty of the arm, of the hands and, of the neck are advantageously displayed in playing of the lute. The eyes are employed only in looking upon the company...Nothing represents so well the consort of angelical choirs and give[s] more foretastes of heavenly joys and of everlasting happiness. For the advantages of marriage, how many bachelors and maids have we seen advanced by this agreeing harmony. (quoted in Craig-McFeely 2002, 304)

Fig. 41. Lute Player (1635-36) by Valentin de Boulogne. The Metropolitan Museum of Art, public domain.

19.　1600, AND WHAT FOLLOWED

There was a good reason for the ongoing parallel development and shared history of the oud/lute, which was that it was played so widely. 1600 is a useful date to use to survey the main geographical regions in which it was played—the Persian, Ottoman, Arab, and European realms—and trace in broad terms what happened in each of these in the subsequent centuries. Once again, there are remarkable parallels between the continents.

In 1600, Persia was under the Safavid Dynasty (1522–1722), and from miniatures of the time we can identify ouds in the hands of players, along with other instruments such as *ney, qanun, chang,* and *kamancha.* Sources from the preceding Timurid Empire (with the capital at Herat until 1507) reveal several oud players by name—Qul Muhammad, who also played *gyaychak* and composed, Shaykhi, who also played *gyaychak* and *ney*, and Husayn Udi, who also sang (Feldman 1996, 41–42). However, during the Safavid period, a new style of musical ensemble emerged that favored the *tar* and the *santur.* These gradually reshaped the Persian tradition, promoting a focus on high, clear resonances and the abandonment—or near abandonment—of *barbat, chang,* and *qanun* by the end of the 1600s (During 2005, 88). This was a cultural shift that was part of a broad interest in creating a new style of music, and surely was connected to a desire to craft a Persian cultural sphere that was distinct from those of the Ottoman and Arab worlds, with

whom there were ongoing territorial battles in some regions. Just a couple of illustrations suggest the oud was occasionally played even in the early nineteenth century, but it was not until the late twentieth century that it was once again any kind of focus for Iranian musicians. We will revisit this in Chapter 30.

Fig. 42. Khamsa, Tabriz, 1539–1543. MS showing a barbat player in Iran. British Library, Or. 2265, f.77v.

In 1600, the oud was probably still a core player in the Ottoman court ensemble, which was very similar to that of the Persian court ensemble. Ottoman explorer Evliya Çelebi (1611–1682), who maintained a travelogue over a forty-year period and published it in his *Seyâhatnâme* (Book of Travel), noted six oud players by name, the leading player among whom was likely Persian (Acem Avvad Mehemmed Aga), which reminds us how indebted the Ottoman tradition was to the Persian one, and how many Persian musicians had historically been part of the Ottoman musical sphere (Feldman 1996, 133). From documents dating back to 1525, we can see that oud players had some prestige, as the two at the court were rather well paid (Feldman 1996, 62ff.). Also, the oud was always dignified by its use in the cultivated, "art" traditions, whether in ensembles or accompanying the voice. However, just as in the Persian Empire, the court gradually set the oud aside, as part of a move to create a new cultural sphere that was distinct from Persian and broader Islamic traditions. By around 1650 it had vanished, replaced by the long-necked *tanbur,* which was tentatively joined by instruments not associated with Islam—the *viola d'amore* and (from the Greek-speaking world) the lyre (Feldman 1996, 127). Numerous changes took place at the time, consolidating what was to become the Ottoman court tradition.

Despite its absence from the court, it is clear that the oud was still played within regions ruled by the Ottomans through the eighteenth and nineteenth centuries (more on this in Chapter 32). Perhaps it was also played in domestic or other more modest settings in Istanbul, but most obviously it was a constant part of North African and Arab traditions. This is clear from visitors' reports to the region such as that of Thomas Shaw, an English cleric who was a chaplain in Algiers in the mid-eighteenth century and published a report on his travels through Tunisia, Syria, Egypt, and the Arabian Peninsula in 1838. He wrote of the North African population of Algiers (he referred to them as Moors, distinct from Arabs and Turks), "They have the ouds, or *bass double stringed lute*, bigger than our viol, that is touched with a *plectrum*, besides several smaller *gittar* (or *quetaras*, according to their pronunciation), of different size each of them tuned an *octave* higher than another [italics by Shaw]" (Shaw 1738, 203).

Edward Lane's account of his encounters in Egypt in the 1820s includes a remark that cements its longstanding significance: "This has been for many centuries the instrument most commonly used by the best Arab musicians, and is celebrated by numerous poets" (Lane 1860, 368). The Damascene historian, theorist, and oud player Mikhail Mashaqah (1800–1888) left us a detailed account of the oud in his Treatise on Modern Arab Music, which is testimony to its fundamental role (Smith and Meshakah 1847).

The year 1600 is just one year in the golden period of the lute in Europe, where it had immense popularity for several centuries in "consorts" (ensembles) of lutes, accompanying the voice, and as a solo instrument. More than 30,000 individual lute pieces that date back to before 1800 are preserved in manuscripts and printed lute books, as well as in other books for worship, dance, history, theory, tutors, individual sheets, and iconography. Luthiers experimented in making larger instruments with more courses of strings to extend the range (8, 9, 10, 11, and more), which led also to the invention of even more substantial instruments with extended necks and a second pegbox, accommodating fourteen courses (sometimes fifteen or even nineteen). These, and their variations, are referred to as theorboes, archlutes, a German Baroque lute, and an angelique.

Europeans seem to have felt the need, just like Persians and Ottomans, to redefine themselves vis-à-vis "others" in this period, but they did not initially turn away from the lute with this intention. Instead, while asserting their purely Hellenic cultural roots, they claimed the lute was a close relative of ancient Greek instruments and a substitute for the Orphic lyre. This erased the lute's relationship with the Islamic world. Similarly, while asserting its aptness for the Orphic tradition of musical inspiration, Europeans chose to ignore the long history of Arabic poetry and storytelling with oud. Nevertheless, by 1750 it had been all but wiped out by keyboard instruments—the spinet, clavichord, harpsichord, and finally the fortepiano.

A PERFORMER ON THE 'OOD.

Fig. 43. Line drawing from Edward Lane's An Account of the Manners and Customs of the Modern Egyptians (1860).

20. 1800, AND WHAT FOLLOWED

For very different reasons, 1800 is also an important moment because it marks the beginning of a new type of movement of ouds into Europe. When Napoleon invaded Egypt in 1798, he took not only his army but also 159 men who formed a "Commission of the Sciences and Arts" to conduct research in the country. One of them was musician and writer Guillaume André Villoteau (1759–1839), who collected instruments to bring back home to France, including an oud. As we saw above, his careful description survives within the ten huge volumes of text (each one measuring 43.5 cm x 28 cm) (Villoteau 1813), and an illustration can be found within the thirteen volumes of images (even larger, at 70 cm x 53 cm) of Napoleon's *Description de l'Égypte* (Volume II of the series *État moderne*).

Another fundamental date to consider is 1831, when Muhammed Ali led Egypt into its military campaign to take control of greater Syria, which had been ruled at arm's length by the Ottomans since 1517. The resulting occupation, and Turko-Egyptian military conflicts that ended only in 1841, fired up divisions that were an inherent part of the local feudal system. The conflicts paved the way for European involvement and, ultimately, Anglo-French rivalry that would dominate the region for a century. In short, the Egyptian regime supported peasant groups to rebel against the feudal establishment, and Great Britain stepped

in to support and protect the feudal lords, a move that was also in opposition to the Ottoman Sultan Mahmud II, who sought to dismantle the current system. In time, each of the various sects and factions in the province of Mount Lebanon aligned themselves with a European "protector," and their differences became vehicles and then policy instruments for European powers.

This was not originally a religious divide. Until Egyptian rule, Druze feudal lords had had the loyalty of both Christian and Druze tenants, and even in the 1840s, loyalties intersected rather than overlapped with religion. (Christian Maronites fought against both Druzes and Greek Orthodox Christians in the 1840s, for instance.) But in time, France's traditional role (since 1536) of protector of the Catholic Church under the Ottomans led it to be aligned with anti-feudal interests, while Great Britain bolstered feudal groups in order to secure a presence that could hold France in check. Increasingly, regional conflict, labeled as sectarian, was what gave France and Great Britain the rationale for their direct intervention.

This increasingly interventionist context was the one in which Europeans began building museums back home, which were monuments to their power to organize how the world was understood. When they bought or took objects such as instruments, it was in the interest of research, extending their capacity to define the world with concepts and institutions. It is thanks to this colonial collecting and educational drive that we still have repositories of historical objects from around the world in museums of the Global North. The historical greed and violence that facilitated their growth shapes debates today about who has the right to say what they mean, and whether the items should be returned to the countries from which they were brought. It is not so much about the individual objects (how much a European collector paid for an oud, for instance), but about the broad state interventions that shaped the context in which such purchases could take place. All these matters take us rapidly into the next section, and the oldest ouds we know about.

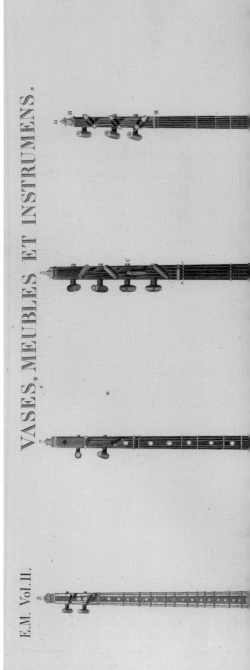

Fig. 44. Instruments identified by Napoleon's team in Egypt, published in Description de l'Égypte, État moderne, Volume II, plate AA.

INSTRUMENS ORIENTAUX A CORDE CONNUS EN ÉGYPTE.

Part V:

OUDS ALONG THE
ROUTES OF EMPIRE

21.   NAPOLEON AND THE OLDEST OUDS IN EUROPE TODAY

Setting aside the case of Napoleon we looked at in Chapter 20, it is difficult to make much of a link between a European leader and an oud. Nevertheless, the oldest surviving ouds today are with us precisely because of struggles between state powers—Ottomans, Egyptians, and Europeans. Power struggles affected everything that was thought and said about instruments throughout the nineteenth and twentieth centuries. Even today, labels such as "Turkish" or "Iraqi" for ouds are territorial and competitive in related ways.

The oldest surviving oud is one example. It was acquired by Belgian musician and scholar François-Joseph Fétis (1784–1871) to support his research and should have been very helpful indeed. However, he viewed all the instruments he acquired through the racist European propaganda of the time. Music from outside Europe was imagined to lag behind, because people from other continents were assumed to be on a lower level of development than Europeans. As a result, just like other European collectors and scholars, Fétis focused on the instruments' supposed potential to reveal cultural production in an earlier stage of humanity (Fétis 1869; Pasler 2004, 26ff.).

Figs. 45 and 46. Egyptian oud, pre-1839. Photo credit David San Millán. Courtesy of the Musical Instruments Museum, Brussels.

According to the note he made in his *Histoire générale de la musique*, Fétis had asked the Belgian consul in Alexandria, Étienne Zizinia (1794–1868), to help him realize his ambition to understand music from all over the world (Beckles Willson 2016b). Zizinia was obliging, so Fétis became the owner of a substantial collection. Was a racist mindset what led him to ignore the actual oud he had acquired completely when he wrote about it? Whatever the reason, he relied on existing publications in his description, drawing on Villoteau's commentary about the oud brought by Napoleon's team and a Latin translation of writing by philosopher al-Farabi. Even the measurements Fétis provided were those of the instrument that arrived in Europe earlier, published by Villoteau (Abdallah 2017, 172).

The oud he had acquired is far larger than what we are used to seeing today. The length from the base to the top of the neck is 73.5 cm, while the body depth (23.5 cm) is more than half the widest part of the face, which measures 40.1 cm; the vibrating string length is 63.7 cm. A useful comparison could be made with the family of ouds built for Mustafa Said by luthier Albert Mansur, mentioned in Chapter 7 above. It is a little shorter than the largest of these, but perhaps it served a "bass" function, as does the one in Said's ensemble.

We have no way of knowing exactly when, where, and by whom it was made, because it was not until much later in the nineteenth century that Egyptian luthiers began labeling their instruments. But it exemplifies the seven-course instrument mentioned in writings from the Ottoman capital of Istanbul in the fifteenth century (Chapter 9). Given that it was likely made around the same time as the oud Villoteau brought to Europe, Villoteau's description is useful as a comparison, as are the writings of contemporary historian, theorist, and oud player Mikhail Meshakah of Damascus (1800–1888) (Smith and Meshakah 1847). Villoteau's and Meshakah's commentaries are in accord with one another on the tuning of the main four courses, which in the terminology of the Ottoman times were *rast, nawa, dugah,* and *usheiran* (G, D, A, and E, as shown in fig. 14).[7] According to Meshakah, only these four courses were played very much, while the others served as resonators. This helps explain why, on the seven-course example we have, the outer strings lie partially off the fingerboard.

These writers describe slightly different tuning for the outer strings. Villoteau refers to *buselik* (used for string VI) and *irak* (VII), while the bass string is *qaba nawa*, forming an octave with the higher *nawa*. This *qaba nawa* provided the foundational tone of the Arab and Ottoman modal systems, and according to Villoteau was placed on the right. Meshakah's tuning is differently inflected: *sikah* rather than *buselik* (string VI), and *nihuft* rather than *irak* (string VII), and there also octave displacements of

ROUTES OF EMPIRE

105

other strings. Finally, the bass is lowered to *jiharkah* (C) rather than *qaba nawa*. The tuning of this deepest string was, and is today, typically adjusted to support the *maqam* being played; the differences in the micro-tuning of strings VI and VII are harder to explain but may be consequences of differing theoretical traditions on which each of the writers drew, and different reference points for the basic *maqam* to which the specified tuning was suited. In each case the result is an instrument very narrow in range in comparison with the five-course instruments in circulation.

The instrument received by Fétis has no frets tied to the neck in its surviving state (unlike the one described by Meshakah). It is only very lightly braced inside, and without any dowel or dovetail joint linking the neck to the body. This aspect of the construction suggests it was not tuned tightly. The narrow range and the cross-tuning – better suited for work with resonances than elaborate melody – reinforce the idea that it was an accompanying instrument, used within an ensemble of others that could be played with more agility. It seems much rougher in craftsmanship than the oud illustrated in Villoteau's volume, which may tell us something about the places in which they were each played. Perhaps the one collected by Villoteau was for the court or other nobility? Was the one received by Fétis an oud for more modest private homes, or an oud played on the street?

These days, the join point between oud neck and body marks the point at two-thirds of the resonating part of the string , which creates the perfect fifth (the third harmonic) when pressed. At the time when Meshakah was writing, ouds had a mark to show this point on the neck, and in our example in Brussels, as well as in the picture of Villoteau's oud, we see how the wood of the face extended onto the neck, so the change in wood color marks this point. The extension of the face onto the fingerboard was a feature of some Renaissance lutes. Two other features of the oud seem to indicate further connections with the lute: the straight pegbox and the large end-clasp at the base of the instrument, where the twenty-three ribs join. Could there have been a direct influence from Europe? Or an influence from Europe that arrived in some way to Egypt having first passed through the Ottoman court? Or was the influence still in the other direction, from east to west? As Section IV revealed, it can be unhelpful to write the history of instruments within the borders established by states and their armies. The threads connecting the regions are stronger than the divisions between them.

On Fétis' death, his son Edouard sold his instrument collection to the Belgian state, and it was part of the core of the musical instrument collection established at the Brussels Royal Music Conservatory in 1877. In subsequent years, state collections of musical instruments became a trend in Europe within the more general expansion of museums. They grew as a consequence of instruments being played and displayed at international trade fairs such as those held in London (1851, 1862) and Paris (1855, 1867).

Behind all such collections were gestures of international diplomacy and exchange that saw instruments and other objects gifted between rulers attending the fairs. In the case of England, at least, they were also part of a drive for national education led by the crown, specifically Prince Albert, consort to Queen Victoria. The newly founded museum complex in London's South Kensington was to be an encyclopedic repository of objects from around the world, serving the educational development of the British public. The complex is still there today, including the Natural History Museum (1864), the Science Museum (1909), Royal Albert Hall (1867), Royal College of Music (1883), and the Victoria and Albert Museum (founded as the Kensington Museum in 1857)—among others (Robertson 2004). There was a deeply racist profiling that shaped all these collections, because ultimately this could help garner support for the increasingly interventionist behavior of European powers outside their own territories.

Fig. 47. Egyptian oud, pre-1839. Photo credit David San Millán. Courtesy of the Musical Instruments Museum, Brussels.

22.   THE OLDEST OUDS FROM THE NAHHAT DYNASTY

The oldest surviving oud with a maker's label inside is also the oldest surviving oud made in Syria. Moreover, it is the oldest surviving oud made by a member of a celebrated dynasty of makers, the al-Nahhat family. It was brought to Europe at some point between 1878—when it was made—and 1894, when Sir George Donaldson (1845–1925) gifted it to the Prince of Wales in London. Donaldson was an English dealer in antique furniture, tapestries, paintings, drawings, and sculpture. He was one of many well-to-do individuals in Europe who sought to define themselves through their possessions, buying (often aesthetically beautiful) things in order to extend their personal prestige. Donaldson was also an amateur violinist (owning a Stradivarius) and had a particular taste for decorative musical instruments. When he gave the oud away, it was part of a collection of 166 objects, mainly instruments, that were to form the core of a museum within the new building of London's Royal College of Music, of which the Prince of Wales was president (Wells 2007).

Donaldson's catalog offers us no hint of how he acquired the oud, but he likely came across it while living in France, or while traveling in Italy (Donaldson 1899). The bulk of his instruments were made in Europe, and the compiler of the catalog, Alfred James Hipkins (1826-1903), was as careless as Fétis in his handling of instruments with which he wasn't familiar. Nevertheless, the oud had special treatment. One illustration in the catalog shows a group identified as "Oriental," and listed individually as "rabab," "Indian fiddle," "Kasso, African Fiddle (Senegambia)," "Koto," "Sarange," "Persian Fiddle," and "Senegalese Drum." The oud, on the other hand, is pictured beside two Italian lutes of the sixteenth and eighteenth centuries and identified as "Persian," from the seventeenth century. So in Hipkins's imagination, the European lute and Persian "lutes" could be brought together and held apart from his "Oriental" category.

Donaldson made his gift to the Royal College of Music with certain conditions attached to it. It was to be housed in a particular room, which he himself would design for display, providing all the necessary alterations and furnishings at his own expense (Wells 2007, 109ff.). So he had the ceiling fitted with cedar coffering and carved supports that were variously gilded and painted; there were mosaic paintings, crimson silk wall hangings, carved wooden doorways, and stone columns erected within the rooms. Furniture of the Italian Renaissance—tables and coffers—formed part of the setting, as did windows that combined old stained-glass panels with newly commissioned ones involving the coat of arms of Albert, Prince of Wales. Musical instruments were gathered in glass cases.

This setting was not the first that Donaldson had arranged publicly for his collection. He had already designed spaces for several exhibitions, including rooms within the International Inventions Exhibition at the Royal Albert Hall in 1885. In each place, he created lavish historical settings, with instruments within them either as primary foci or adding to the generally elegant effect. Replete with display cabinets, these spaces were extensions of Donaldson's home environment, for this too he curated several rooms historically.

The oud was unquestionably a match for the elegance Donaldson so cherished, because the delicacy of its crafting is indebted to the tradition of woodcarving for which Damascus is celebrated. It would be tempting to imagine that it was made for him, catering to European tastes for the decorative. However, the pickguard and face are marked by indentations caused by playing, which suggest Donaldson acquired it from a player. The maker identifies himself as Yusif al-Nahhat on the label, but we lack any documentary evidence to understand whether this Yusif was older than al-Nahhat brothers (Ikhwan al-Nahhat), Rufan and Abdo, who set up their workshop in Damascus in 1880. The name of their father was George Yusif, and given the naming habits of Christian families it is possible that Yusif was *his* father. But we cannot be sure.

The proportions and shape of the instrument are in line with those of instruments the al-Nahhat brothers made in the same period, but the two-layered construction of the bowl (seventeen ribs inside and a further bowl made entirely of filaments) has not been seen on any other ouds. Where the face reaches the neck there is a bone ornament often referred to as an "almond" (*luza* in Arabic), a larger version of which has been placed at the base of the instrument where the ribs meet. The pegbox is curved and decorated with inlay, its twelve bone pegs inlaid with traditional "eyes" warding off evil (Othman Hassan 2016a).

There is another surviving oud made by this Yusif al-Nahhat, held in the museum at the Royal Northern College of Music in Manchester. This was similarly part of a private collection, this time belonging to a musician and teacher in Manchester called Henry Watson (1846–1911). Watson seems to have had a humble start in life but made a step-by-step shift from errand boy in a Blackburn music shop to Professor of Piano at the Royal Manchester College of Music (picking up a Ph.D. from Cambridge University along the way) and amassing a significant collection of instruments. He left his large library and collection to the college (now Royal Northern College of Music), but without any information about how he acquired the oud (Royal Northern College of Music 2010).

It is just as remarkable as the earlier instrument but for different reasons. The elegance of the external finishing is just as striking, and the rosette is exceptionally ornate, with a delicate symmetrical design of loops, arcades, hearts, and fleurs-de-lis, along with a gold (perhaps gilt) center in which eight scrolls surround a glass gem. But most extraordinary is the inside of the bowl, which has several layers of paper glued to the surface, including not just the label stating that it was made in Damascus in 1874, but also pictures of a European-style picnic.

Fig. 49a. Part of internal decorations of Oud by Yusif al-Nahhat, 1874. Courtesy of the Royal Northern College of Music, Manchester.

The inside decoration presents us with a lot of questions. Just fourteen years before this oud was made, Europeans had begun to make their presence felt in the region in very problematic ways.

Fig. 48. Oud by Yusif al-Nahhat, 1874. Courtesy of the Royal Northern College of Music, Manchester.

First, the Europeans intervened, ostensibly to try to calm a civil war. This had begun as a peasant revolt against feudal oppression but turned into a conflict between opposing religious groups, thanks to sponsorship by different foreign powers. France led the intervention, responding to the 1523 treaty according to which it had a duty to protect Christians of the Ottoman Empire, and remained in Syria for over a year. Just as in previous decades, the French sided with the Egyptians (in their attempt to take control from the Ottomans), whereas the British sided with the Ottomans. The conflict between them continued, with the British supporting the Druze of Syria and Lebanon. By the end of the war, over 12,000 Christians and Druze had died, and an autonomous Maronite Christian region was established in the province of Mount Lebanon. The Ottoman powers' desire to remain in control of its enormous empire was being severely challenged by regional nationalism, along with European fueling of sectarian difference.

In this light, the picture of a picnic in the oud seems unlikely to have been part of the original design. Or was it a parody of upper-class European society? Or just chance use of paper from a European magazine? Or could it all have been added later, in England? But for what purpose? And the fact that Yusif al-Nahhat's label is stuck onto the picture suggests he himself put it there. Whatever the motivation for lining the oud with these designs, they remind us that even by looking inside instruments we can find new ways to think about the deep and often painful links between Europe and the Arab world.

Fig. 49b. Part of internal decorations of Oud by Yusif al-Nahhat, 1874. Courtesy of the Royal Northern College of Music, Manchester.

23.   DIPLOMACY AND THE OUD

While a direct link is difficult to trace between al-Nahhat ouds and the various imperial powers attempting to shape the region, the case is different for an oud that Ismail Pasha, the khedive of Egypt, gifted to London's Kensington Museum in 1867 (Beckles Willson 2016a). The French state had mounted its second Exposition Universelle in Paris that year, and it involved not only massive displays of French industry but also exhibits from other nations. Many of the displays presented musical instruments, and the Egyptian one must have included an oud, or even a group of live musicians playing. Following the exposition, Ismail Pasha donated at least twenty-five instruments to the South Kensington Museum in London. The musician, writer, and instrument collector Carl Engel probably negotiated this gift, as he was doing some shopping at the Exposition and was developing an instrument collection for the museum.

Fig. 50. Oud arbi donated to the South Kensington Museum by Ismail Pasha, the khedive of Egypt. Photo credit by David San Millán. Copyright Horniman Museum and Gardens (object number M24.8.56/95).

Just as we saw in the case of Fétis, the instruments didn't necessarily lead to an understanding of their cultures of origin. When they arrived in London, they were entered into the South Kensington museum's records, and the oud was initially categorized as a "mandoline," only later corrected to oud. Seven years later Engel published a catalog of the collection, stating that ten of Ismail Pasha's other gifts were percussion instruments (listed as "tabl," "darbouka," "nakrazan"), eight were wind instruments ("arghool," "whistle," "negro trumpet"), and five were lyres ("kissar" and "negro harp"); there was also a "rebab." Regarding the oud, Engel provided information about what ouds were "usually" and "generally" like by drawing from Edward Lane's *An Account of the Manners and Customs of the Modern Egyptians*, which describes and illustrates an oud of seven strings (Engel 1870, 142; Lane 1860, 368). But the South Kensington museum's oud was, for anyone looking closely, at odds with Lane's description. Engel himself observed that it had four double courses of strings and was three feet long and one foot wide.

Today we know that this type of instrument is an integral part of traditions in Algeria, Morocco, and Tunisia, and is variously termed *oud arbi, oud tunsi,* or *quwaytara* (or *kuitra, kwitra*) (Morra 2018, 69ff.). In Tunisia, it is usually referred to as *oud arbi* to distinguish it from the widely played Egyptian-style oud known as *oud sharqi*. It has eleven ribs, and a piece of animal skin smoothes the join to the face, which is made from six pieces of wood, with three geometrically designed rosettes carved out of it. It is very likely that the strings were originally tuned in the characteristic North African way, in which the lowest- and highest-pitched strings are the first and second strings from the left, while the next along to the right are between them in pitch, typically D, d^1 G, c^1 in Helmholtz notation.

Fig. 51. Rosette of Oud arbi donated to the South Kensington Museum by Ismail Pasha, the khedive of Egypt. Photo credit by David San Millán. Copyright Horniman Museum and Gardens (object number M24.8.56/95).

We have no way of knowing who made the instrument, although nineteenth-century makers are thought to have been practicing musicians who were part of the Jewish community of Tunisia. This particular rosette pattern can be found in twentieth-century ouds from Tunisia and is used today by makers such as Ridha Jandoubi and Faisal Ṭwiri; it has a nominal association with the legendary player Khamais Tarnan (1894–1964) (Morra 2018, 79). Tunisian musicians played in ensembles at several of the European and North American trade fairs in the nineteenth century, which may explain why several of these instruments can be found in museum collections today, such as in Berlin, Brussels, Lille, Nantes, New York, Nuremberg, Paris, and Vienna.[8]

This oud was displayed for some years in the South Kensington Museum, which later became the Victoria and Albert Museum, but we have little idea about the exact exhibit context. The museum was shaped by a state concern with industry and education; it was essentially a design school whose collections were open to the public and used by learned societies. When the oud arrived, staff logged it within the "woodwork" department, suggesting that instruments of different materials may have served particular schools (Beckles Willson 2016a). They would thus have been distributed around the museum as samples of and models for a range of artistic work, rather than as vehicles for music making. In 1873, just as he became responsible for both arts and science education, Major-General John Donnelly stated that the collections were "essentially the apparatus for teaching" (Robertson 2004, 8).

Fig. 52. Oud arbi donated to the South Kensington Museum by Ismail Pasha, the khedive of Egypt. Photo credit by David San Millán. Copyright Horniman Museum and Gardens (object number M24.8.56/95).

24. FROM THE EDGES OF EMPIRE

We may be used to thinking of capital cities as centers for the creation of ideas and wealth that spread outward to the provinces. But movement in the opposite direction is frequently what the center relies on for new ideas, just as shifts in concentrations of power and wealth play their part. The revival of oud making and oud playing in late-nineteenth-century Istanbul is most likely a result of such movements, as well as changing relationships between the capital and other regional and even intercontinental concentrations of power.

Fig. 53. Oud by Iskender Qudmany. Photo by the author.

At the level of the Istanbul court there was a newly changing relationship with Egypt, as Ismail Pasha—the new khedive—negotiated the authority to make reforms over the administrative region for which he was responsible. Among the gifts sent from Egypt to Istanbul around 1863–ostensibly for Bezmiâlem Valide Sultan, mother of Sultan Abdulmejid—was an ensemble of Egyptian musicians. It included two *qanun* players, a *rebab* player, singers, and an oud player whose name appears in court records as "Udcu Mehmed Ömer Efendi" or "Misir'li Ömer Efendi." Egyptians remained in the court records for some years, with very respectable salaries and no doubt considerable influence on the aesthetics of court.

More informal movement from the provinces to the capital shaped music life in less rarefied communities. Oud player Misirli Ibrahim Effendi visited the city from Cairo to play in nightclubs, and three Qudmany brothers—Selim, Tawfik, and Iskender—moved to Istanbul from Damascus at the start of the century, variously making ouds, performing, teaching music, and running a music publishing house and music shops. Ouds in numerous genre pictures and postcards of the time closely resemble Qudmany instruments that survive today: see figures 53, and 54a-c below, and compare the ouds with figure 32a in Chapter 11 above.

The Qudmany brothers were indebted to the crafting traditions of Damascus, where delicately inlaid wooden furniture and decorative objects had long been made in workshops and exported regionally and internationally. Typically instruments from the Syrian oud-making tradition have a body made with a particular shape; at the base

are frequently very light, thanks to their very thin ribs. The one in figure 32a, made around 1904 by Shamli Tevfik and Shamli Iskender Kutmanyzade, (their Turkish names), has a string length of 62 cm, which is long for the ouds of Istanbul that we encounter more frequently, but characteristic of Syrian ouds. The rosette is also typical for Damascus at the time, just as the maple and walnut bridge is characteristic of instruments from Damascus and Cairo (Othman Hassan 2016d; 2016c).

it is rounded toward the face, curving inward slightly to allow the right arm to move comfortably around the end of the instrument. For this design, every rib must be bent to a different form. Qudmany ouds

Figs. 54a, 54b and 54c. Vintage pictures. No copyright traced.

By the beginning of the twentieth century, when the Qudmanys arrived in Istanbul, one local luthier had begun making ouds with significant success. This was Emmanuel Venios (1845–1915), a member of the Greek-speaking minority of the city, who worked initially as a furniture-polisher. He may well have begun by making lavtas, the fretted lutes that were played widely in clubs, and he emerged from what was perhaps a small but active community of Greek instrument makers (surviving names include Izmitli (1870–?) and Kapudagli Ilya Kanakis (1870–1930), Kosti Karagöz (1870–?), and Vasil (1875–1915)). Known professionally as Manol, Venios established a workshop with numerous collaborating craftsmen, which enabled him to produce large numbers of ouds and to train apprentices who went on to make ouds in their own names. His students included future oud makers in the Turkish community such as Hamza (1884-1915), Mustafa Usta (1885–1935), and Murat Sümbül (1884–1960); and their students continued the lineage, including Hadi Erogluer (1910–1990) and Teoman Kaya (b. 1934, who became an apprentice under Murat Sümbül at the age of twelve) (Üngör 2000).

Fig. 55. Oud made in 1908 by Emmanuel Venios (Manol), owned by Ara Dinkjian.

Another important strand in oud production developed in the Armenian minority. In fact it is Armenian names that proliferate in the earliest phase of revived oud making in Istanbul: Baron Baronak (1834–1900), Uzunyan Artin Haruyun (1845–?), Mihran Keresteciyan (1865–1940), and most importantly, Kirkor Kahyayan (1875–1933) and his son Leon, along with students Onnik Karipyian Kücüküner (1900–?) and Levon Bogosyan Gözenoglu (1900–1979) (Üngör 2000). With such a profusion of oud making among distinct but interweaving communities, each with their own histories of instrument making, it is not surprising that there were some new developments in crafting. This can be seen clearly in two Armenian ouds shown in figure 56, one from Beirut (Leon Istanbuli) and one from Istanbul (Ali Galip). While Istanbuli's oud has the near-spherical Arab model for the lower part of the body, that of Galip has a flattened base area—which became typical among ouds made by Greeks and Armenians in turn-of-the-century Istanbul. The face of the Galip instrument has three sound holes, rather than one. The vibrating string length is generally shorter—around 58 cm rather than 60 cm—and the body is significantly shallower, even while often quite wide. The sound is distinct, in general having a thinner, less "bass-y" resonance.

Fig. 56 Two ouds by Armenian makers. Instrument on the left by Leon Istanbuli (workshop in Beirut, date not visible); instrument on the right by Ali Galip (1920), whose workshop was in Istanbul.

And yet this style of instrument had not entirely displaced others. To grasp this fully, we could look at a very modest instrument, which found its way into the Swedish Museum of Performing Arts (Scenkonstmuseet) in Stockholm. This museum was founded as the Musikhistoriska museet in 1899, following the Stockholm Art and Industry Exhibition of 1897, and opened to the general public in 1901. Unfortunately, the museum has no record of how the oud got there, but the current curator, Eva Olandersson, guesses it arrived between the late 1970s and 1990 (Beckles Willson 2016f).

The label of this oud indicates that the maker, Mustafa, was a student registered as "no. 77" at a vocational school of arts in Adana, the third-largest city in Turkey today. The date of the making is noted in the Rumi calendar, which translates to the Gregorian as 14 March 1907. So it falls within the reign of Ottoman Sultan Abdülhamid II (1876–1909), a ruler who established many vocational schools of arts and handcrafts. Nevertheless, the oud does not demonstrate a strong influence from the Greek and Armenian makers of Istanbul. The face of the oud has only one sound hole, and the rosette is glued inside without any border or inset lining, which is typical for the Aleppian luthier George Hayek (Othman Hassan 2016f). The simple palm motive and floral tendrils of the pickguard also recall some early instruments from Aleppo.

The bridge, on the other hand, is a type that is more typical of Cairene and Damascene ouds, just as the "almond"—a decoration marking the end of the neck where it joins the body—is in line with Damascus ouds. So, whether for reasons of economy, taste, or cultural affiliation, this oud suggests that Arab ouds were used as models at this school. Adana was once on an important trade route to Syria and had a significant proportion of Arabic-speaking people in its population at the time, just as it does now.

Fig. 57b. Label from inside oud by "Mustafa," Adana 1907. Photo by the author. Swedish Museum of Performing Arts in Stockholm (Sweden), object inventory number X5058.

Fig. 57a. Oud by "Mustafa," Adana 1907. Courtesy of the Swedish Museum of Performing Arts in Stockholm (object inventory number X5058).

25. NATIONAL OUDS?

World War I and the subsequent breakup of the Ottoman Empire saw a brutal redrawing of the map, the notorious "population exchange" of Greeks and Turks, and immense bloodshed— including a systematic genocide of Armenians and other Christians by the Ottoman "Committee of Union and Progress." One consequence was the forced migration of large numbers of people, and the establishment of immigrant populations elsewhere (on this more in Chapter 32). Another was the consolidation of post-imperial and post-colonial nations such as Greece and Turkey, and also Iraq. Nationalized institutions and nationalist thinking affected instrument making and music making strongly, even while the legacy of the multi-ethnic Ottoman Empire frequently remained at the core of society.

The case of Turkey is particularly clear in this respect. Despite the ethnic cleansing, Armenian oud makers were still numerous in the Istanbul of the new Republic of Turkey as well as in the new administrative capital, Ankara. Significant names include Ali Galip Sözen (b.1890), Hacik Atamian, Artin Atikiyan, Artin Hatun, and Onnik Karipyian Kücüküner (b. 1900), who was making ouds into the 1960s (Üngör 2000). However, the Turkish Republic formed new relationships with Europe, and new institutions emerged that were modeled on European systems of education and industry. These triggered numerous changes in instrument making and branding.

Most obvious was the development of a formalized system of instrument production, seen in an instrument manufacturing workshop founded at the Ankara State Conservatory in 1936, led by the German Heinz Schafrat, who stayed in Ankara until the beginning of World War II (Tetik Isik 2013, 278). One of his students, Mithat Arman (1910–1987), went on to develop the Instrument Manufacturing Workshop at the Gazi Institute for Education in Ankara. This functioned as the Department of Instrument Manufacturing until 1943 when it closed. Shortly afterward, a Department of Instrument Manufacturing was established at the Technical Teacher Training School in Ankara, and this eventually moved to the Ankara State Conservatory. Arman taught there alongside Turkish luthier colleagues, and also luthiers from Europe such as Christian Schertel and Étienne Vatelot.

This new "academic" line of instrument building in Turkey was shaped by the new state's interest in the industrialized production of instruments and in particular those of the western classical traditions such as pianos. Eventually it would feed into the mass production of ouds. However, it also brought expertise in craftsmanship, which fed into the techniques of instrument crafting already being produced locally. Among Arman's students in Ankara was one Cafer Açın (1939–2012), who

THE
OUD

Fig. 58. Mass-produced ouds and baǧlamas.

was fundamental to the development of oud making in Istanbul (Tetik Isik 2013, 280ff.). He taught initially at the Istanbul Turkish Music State Conservatory (TMSC) and subsequently directed the Department of Instrument Manufacturing when the conservatory was affiliated with Istanbul Technical University (ITU).

Numerous instrument makers today refer to Açın as their teacher, or a major influence, including some of Istanbul's most celebrated oud makers, such as Mustafa Copçuoglu and Ramazan Calay, who work by hand in small workshops. The ouds of luthier Faruk Türünz were particularly sought after and widely exported once they were taken up by oud virtuoso and teacher Yurdal Tokcan. Fundamentally, the work of these distinguished luthiers consolidates and—to a certain extent—standardizes the styles of late Ottoman ouds made in the Greek and Armenian communities of Istanbul. In general, they are heavier and sturdier than the earlier instruments, but they remain smaller than the typical Arab models and consequently have less bass resonance. They also have a low string "action," so strings are closer to the fingerboard, which tends to make a characteristic buzz associated with the "Turkish" style of playing.

Turkish oud player Necati Çelik playing Sadi Isılay's Muhayyer Kürdi Saz Semaisi

Fig. 59. Two modern Turkish ouds from Istanbul by Faruk Türünz (above) and Ramazan Calay (below). Photo by the author.

The case of Iraq was quite distinct. Iraq was taken over by the British as a "mandate of Mesopotamia" after the Ottoman collapse, but it became an independent kingdom in 1932, under Faisal I, who had been King of Iraq since 1921. Faisal's reign was shaped by a desire to build a modern nation, a project that was extremely fraught, particularly given that the borders drawn by the British took no account of the diverse affiliations of communities inside (Shia and Sunni Arabs, Kurds, Christian Assyrians, Jews, Circassians, and Turkmens, among others). Faisal died suddenly in 1933 and his son Ghazi came to the throne, but it has been claimed that Faisal conceived of the Institute of Fine Arts in Baghdad, established in 1936. Even though it was founded so late, it does seem to emerge from the educational reforms that characterized the time of Faisal's nation-building. The music education that developed there also followed suit.

Nevertheless, three key figures in the music program had benefitted from the traditions of Istanbul. Two of these were luthiers: a father-son team of Iranians, Usta Ali (born in Iran in 1904 but moving to Turkey, where he seems to have studied luthiery) and his son Muhammad Ali (d. 2002) (Beckles Willson and Othman Hassan 2017). Muhammad Ali was born in the 1920s in Lebanon, where the family had relocated by then, likely lured there by the burgeoning and increasingly lively music scene, and moved again with the family to Baghdad in 1935. The third influential figure was Sherif Muhiddin Haydar (also known as Sherif Muhiddin Targan, 1892–1967, mentioned already in Chapter 10), a cellist and an oud player who was brought from Istanbul to direct the music department of the Institute of Fine Arts in 1937. We will explore the work of Sherif Muhiddin in more detail in Chapter 31.

Muhammad Ali and his father, Usta Ali (alias Ali Khanbaba, and known in Iraq as Ali Ajmi in reference to his Iranian origin), were for many years the most sought-after luthiers in Baghdad. Sherif Muhiddin had an oud from their workshop, as did several of his students, including the Iraqi player Salman Shukur (1921–2007), and as mentioned in Chapter 7, Jamil Bashir. Strikingly, these ouds are obviously modeled on instruments of Istanbul rather than those of Syria or Egypt. This may be a result of training Usta Ali had while living in Istanbul, or perhaps he decided to base his constructions on the Istanbul oud of Sherif Muhiddin as a model, which was made by Venios, a member of the Greek-speaking minority of Istanbul, as mentioned above. But while this Ottoman-style oud may have dominated in Iraq for some time, there was another oud model about to emerge.

The context for this oud was what many Iraqis today consider the golden age of modernity, cosmopolitanism, development, and optimism in Iraq, which lasted around a decade starting in 1948. An immense increase in oil revenues and prosperity led to extreme sociopolitical and economic contrasts typical of capitalist expansion and ascent. On the one hand, there was a range of progressive, modernizing currents accompanied by utopian visions for the country. At the same time, thanks to political violence and corruption, the boom disenfranchised much of the population. At the heart of the inequalities were the nationalist vision and practices of the state, which were sectarian even while rhetorically upholding secularism.

A strong desire emerged among visual artists and writers to create a new and identifiably Iraqi culture. The Baghdad Modern Arts Group, founded in 1951, drew on ancient artifacts from the region—Assyrian, Babylonian, Abbasid— to define an "Iraqi" heritage in painting, but using reference points from modern European art. For example, painter Jawad Salim had studied in Paris and Rome. Central to literary developments was *shir al-hurr* (the free verse movement), which can be seen in the work of poets such as Nazik al-Malaika, Badr Shakir al-Sayyab, and Abd al-Wahhab al-Bayati. Crucial to their thinking was an immersion in literature from Europe and the Americas and a strong desire to dismantle traditional forms of the Arabic canon. In line with such thinking, in 1953, the young Munir

Bashir collaborated with Iraqi luthier Mahir Muhammad Fadil Hussain on making a new oud with which he could travel on his first tour out of the country (Beckles Willson 2019b, 474–75). The result seems to have been the first oud with ovular sound holes and a "moon" cut out from the fingerboard on the face of the oud (see figure 34). He took this instrument on his tour, which began in Istanbul.

However, when Bashir traveled on to Beirut from Istanbul, the new oud suffered on the journey, or in the change of climate, and the bridge snapped off, taking part of the face with it. He had hoped to record some songs with Lebanese singer Fairouz and some of his own compositions for the radio. It seems that these projects were both postponed. When he returned to Baghdad, Muhammad Fadel repaired the oud, but in 1957 he also made another instrument, one that had a stronger structure that transformed the sound fundamentally. Most obviously, he built a capacity to cope with high string tension into its design. By securing the strings to the body of the instrument, rather than to a bridge glued on the face, the increasing strain on the face was eliminated. The model is known as a "floating" bridge oud (see figure 60, and also figure 94 in the Afterword).

As we will explore in Chapter 38, Bashir played this oud in the European concerts that kick-started his international career in 1971. Europeans identified it as deeply connected to Iraqi history and the music of the Arab world more broadly. Over time it became known as the "Iraqi oud," appropriate for an instrument that had emerged at a time of intense nationalist modernization and in an increasingly global scope of oud playing.

In recent decades, this oud has become a model and standard at leading educational centers such as the Conservatoire in Damascus, and with a shorter (57 cm) neck also at Bait Al Oud in Abu Dhabi. Frequently the tuning favored by Munir Bashir is also used, one-fourth above standard Egyptian tuning (one tone lower than that of Sherif Muhiddin and Jamil Bashir). Luthiers now make ouds with floating bridges throughout the world, including Belgium, Germany, Greece, Hungary, Lebanon, Syria, Tunisia, Turkey, the US, and likely elsewhere.

Fig. 60. Floating-bridge oud by Muhammad Fadel, 1957.
Photo by the author. Courtesy of Saad Bashir.

26.   INDIVIDUAL WEALTH, GLOBAL ROUTES

Although we live in a very different world today from the one
in which Napoleon set sail for Egypt, ouds remain caught up in
competitions for power and influence. If anything, the connection
between wealth and instruments is more direct than ever. Now the
instruments themselves are part of a market, and it is much larger
than it was when Donaldson was building his collection. It is global.

Two areas in particular allow us to see this. One is the
movement of "cult" ouds, whether made by luthiers from the
legendary al-Nahhat family of Syria or the Greek-speaking Uenios
of Istanbul. Some Egyptian ouds of the early twentieth century
are also collectors' pieces, and they stand out for their slim
bodies, as in the examples shown in figure 3 (Introduction) and
figures 61a and 61b. These historical rarities are traded online
and are sometimes shipped for sums of money that exceed the
annual income of many luthiers.

*Fig. 61a. Oud by Rafia Arazi (1919). From
the collection of Ahmad AlSalhi. Photo by
Fatemah al-Fadel.*

*Fig. 61b. Oud by Numan Rahibe 1912. From
the collection of Ahmad AlSalhi. Photo by
Fatemah al-Fadel.*

The other striking area of global oud trade is production for the luxury goods market. When in 2006 Ritter Instruments made an oud in its Royal series, it sold at auction for $620,000, pushing the oud into lofty new financial territory. The price was partly a result of its materials, but wood was not the deciding component. Rather, it was the 103-carat black diamond, 24-carat gold, and 10,000-year-old ivory.

Just a few years later in 2015, luthier and oud player Wissam Joubran custom-built an oud that incorporated ivory and 24-carat gold, along with rare woods such as Indian rosewood. And in the following year, the workshop of Faruk Türünz presented ouds at an expo in the United Arab Emirates hosted under the patronage of Shaykh Nahayan bin Mabarak al-Nahayan, UAE's Minister of Culture and Knowledge Development. One of these incorporated 14-carat gold decorations.

The expo—strikingly titled "Big Boys Toys"— could be seen as an outgrowth of the world's fairs originating in nineteenth-century Europe. Prestige remains attached to the creation of technologies, and to ownership of objects with lavish decorations. But there are changes that reflect our changed societies. There is the visibility brought about by internet trading. There is the purchasing of new ouds by enormously wealthy individuals, and there is the geographical shift of wealth. While in the nineteenth century Europe could boast a concentration of wealth and private collectors, today there is little doubt that the leaders in high-end oud purchases are individuals in the Gulf States.

Fig. 62. This postage stamp from the UEA suggests a strong adherence to traditional oud playing.

27. MARITIME ROUTES AND OIL EMPIRES

In 1965, I made an instrument that looks like an oud. I took a can of oil from the British company Shell. I opened all the top then I went to a carpentry workshop in San'a. There I took a piece of tunub wood of 80 centimeters, an elongated piece 10 centimeters wide at one end, and just 5 centimeters at the other. I hammered this piece of wood into the top of the can, which was open, and nailed it to the inside. Then I took another piece of wood 60 centimeters long and 5 centimeters wide, which I divided into three equal pieces, and I nailed these three pieces together to make a tailpiece, which I have attached to the handle. Then I bought a set of strings and it made a lute. (al-Nûnû and Lambert 2002, 43 (translation from French by RBW))

This extract from the autobiography of Yemeni musician Yahya al-Nûnû offers an unusual way of thinking about the oud in a region that has changed unrecognizably in the last century, namely the Arabian Peninsula. In the late nineteenth century, the peninsula was part of a maritime economic sphere that connected it with East Africa and West India. But the discovery of oil in Bahrain (1932) and Saudi Arabia (1938) transformed it, attracting the interest of surrounding empires and bringing enormous wealth to all countries except Yemen. The Yemeni al-Nûnû's construction of an oud from a discarded Shell oil can is not only a story of creativity amid hardship, but one with a tragic dimension at its heart.

This is all the more poignant when we think about the musical genre in which the oud is most deeply involved in the rich Gulf countries of Bahrain and Kuwait, namely *saut*, which is indebted to Yemen. *Saut* involves a singer, an oud player, and a violinist, and the drums from Yemen called *mirwas*. Numerous other Yemeni elements imbue *saut*: poetic genres, song structures, rhythmic meters, and concepts used to describe music (Al-Salhi 2016, 125–28).

Maritime movements and migrations led to *saut* being established in the rich Gulf States. Bahraini musician Abdallah al-Faraj (1836–1901) was in India when he learned oud and repertoire from Yemeni musicians who lived there. He was also exposed to aspects of Indian music that remain important to the *saut* enjoyed today in Kuwait, particularly the use of certain vowel sounds. Al-Faraj returned to Kuwait in the 1850s, bringing these Yemeni and Indian riches. Today, *saut* is sung and played primarily by circles of men in private gatherings on the peninsula, particularly Kuwait. The musical role of the oud is to introduce and often link songs, and to support the singer (who is often the oud player himself). While seemingly deeply embedded in rich national cultures, this oud culture is part of a rich history of interaction with mainly coastal neighbors—some of whom now live in great poverty and deprivation.

Al-Faraj even brought the oud itself to the peninsula—although what he brought, which Kuwaitis refer to as the *oud hindi,* is different from the oud played widely today (Al-Salhi 2016, 175). It had a round body carved out of a single piece of wood and a skin on the face, and was played in *saut* until the 1950s. Lambert (2021, 88–95) proposes that this *oud hindi* may have been a *qanbus*, the skin-topped oud referred to as *qanbus* in Yemen. Similar to the description of the *oud hindi*, the *qanbus* is carved out of a single piece of wood and has a skin as the face—connecting us to the earliest short-necked lutes of Central Asia discussed at the start of this book—and it certainly spread widely, in the Hijaz and the Indonesian archipelago, also Malaysia. It may have arrived in these areas directly from Yemen and may even have been part of the spread of Islam on the Malay Peninsula that was happening as early as the fifteenth century. There are documentary traces of its presence in the eighteenth century in both Yemen and India, and its use in Indonesia and Malaysia must have increased with the diaspora of Hadhrami Arabs from Yemen at that time, along with movements of British colonizers in the region (Lambert 2021, 95–96).

Skin-topped short-necked lutes have had to compete—increasingly unsuccessfully—with the more sturdy wooden-topped ouds. In Kuwait, they were almost wiped out by the 1930s (Al-Salhi 2016, 48), and although in Malaysia the terms *gambus* (equivalent to the Yemen term *qanbus*) and oud are used interchangeably, Egyptian and Turkish instruments dominate there too, particularly in urban areas (Kinzer 2017, 57). This may in part be due to Malaysia's increasing connections with oil-rich states, including Saudi Arabia, as the country exploits its own oil resources. Today the oud and *qambus* are instruments of prestige in Malaysia, associated with wealth and Islam.

Qanbus-like instruments in Kenya, Tanzania, and the Comoros remind us of the deep maritime links between the Arabian Peninsula and East Africa. But the introduction of the oud to Sudan, the East African country where it has probably been longest established, was likely a consequence of British rule (Lavin 2017). While controlling Egypt in the late nineteenth century, and anxious to maintain the economic and military benefits of the recently opened Suez Canal, Great Britain reconquered Sudan, quashing the Mahdist State that had ousted the Khedivate of Egypt. The army was partly Egyptian, but also included Syrians and others from the Ottoman region, along with the man said to have become the first Sudanese oud player, Muhammad Tamim. Just down the coast from Sudan in Somalia, the first oud player is thought to have been Abdullahi Qarshe (1924–1994), who most likely learned while living in Yemen, where he was sent to study in 1931. Just a little younger than him, another Somali oud player, Ahmed Ismail Hussein Hudeidi (1928–2020) also grew up in Yemen. Hudeidi (or Xudeydi) was to be an important figure in Somali music nationally and internationally, particularly when he settled in London and was a popular and influential figure among the Somali Diaspora. Hudeidi's very name is a consequence of movement between Yemen and East Africa: it was a family nickname for his grandfather, who traveled by dhow from Somaliland to the eponymous city (in Yemen) to trade (Brinkhurst 2012, 84).

In Sudanese and Somali traditions of oud playing, the instrument is primarily an accompaniment to the voice, but it is also used in mixed ensembles of instruments. Sudanese and Somali compositions tend to develop melodies with *pentatony*, which is characteristic of local repertoires, rather than reproducing Arab *maqam*. ('Pentatony' here refers to five-note scales without semitones, such as the five black keys on a keyboard.)

Similarly, in Malaysia the tendency is to draw the oud into Malay repertoire in which the *gambus* was important. However, there the interest in developing Arab culture is very strong—as can be traced in architecture and tastes in food—and many players learn *maqam* as well. Playing oud in Malaysia is connected to an expression of Islam even if just in the sense of cultural affiliation and identity and not an orthodox or pious sense (Kinzer 2017). Additionally, Malaysian and also Sudanese oud players have been attracted to the soloistic world cultivated at the hubs of Bait Al Oud in Cairo and Abu Dhabi, as we will see in Chapter 31.

These examples reveal some of the main influences in the increasingly regional and even global world of the oud. In East Africa, particularly in countries that are members of the Arab League and the African Union, there are debates about identities along the fracture line of Pan-Arab versus Pan-African. In the recently forged nations of the Arab Peninsula, there are pressures to perform on the stage of international culture, but the debates are ongoing regarding the consequences for local instruments and practices (Danielson 2021; A. K. Rasmussen 2021). In Oman, the Sultanate sponsors an array of musical institutions, many of which depend largely on a workforce from Egypt, Iraq, and elsewhere in the Gulf, and which may—according to several local musicians and thinkers—be to the detriment of local musical identities and careers.

Is a Pan-Arab, outward-facing national identity in the interest of Khaliji (Gulf) repertoire and styles, for instance? (Saudi oud player and composer Abade Al Johar seems to cultivate this approach.) And what about the global lives of women, for whom oud playing is still a contested area? Who decides when Saudi Arabia will see, once again, a female oud player, singer, folklorist, and composer such as Tuha (b. 1934)? With the protection of King Saud ibn Abd al-Aziz from the age of fourteen, Tuha sustained a career that was significant on the Arab peninsula (Campbell 2021, 186–88). But could, or would, an oud-playing woman today take the equivalent steps forward into the public domain?

Fig. 63. Oud by Ahmad Abduljalil, Kuwait, 2012. From the collection of Ahmad AlSalhi. Photo by Fatemah al-Fadel.

Part VI

CHANGING OUD REPERTOIRES

28.   THE OLDEST MUSIC FOR OUD

We saw in earlier chapters how the oud has fascinated not only musicians but also historians and theorists. Thanks to their writing, we have been able to retrace some of the steps in oud construction over time and learn about the social settings in which it was important. However, historians and theorists have served us less well in their musical notation.

An exercise published by Al-Kindi is the oldest precise instruction for oud players that survives. He recommends that the strings be plucked with the thumb and one finger of the *right* hand simultaneously, in different positions, so that the player can learn the intervals (i.e., what two notes sound like played together) (Abdallah 2017, 162–64). This is not a standard practice today, although perhaps it should be! *Kamal Adab al-Ghina* ("The Perfection of Musical Knowledge") by Fatimid writer A-Hasan ibn Ali ibn Ahmad al-Katib (d. eleventh century) lists eighteen playing techniques, including *al-daghdagha*, described as a continuous touching of the strings with the fingers. The other techniques are ways of ornamenting or texturing melodies and rhythms, sometimes with specific picking techniques, such as *jarrat* (dragging the pick across strings) and *tathirat* (stumbling between two strings) (Shiloah 1972, 131ff.; Sawa 2021, 241ff.).

The oldest notated music for oud is found in the writings of musician-theorists Safi al-Din al-Urmawi al-Baghdadi (1216–1294) and his distinguished student Qutb al-Din Mahmoud al-Shirazi (1236–1311) (Wright 1978). Al-Urmawi used the alphabet to represent notes and numerals for rhythmic values that can be grouped into poetic feet. Qutb al-Din and Abd al-Qadir al-Maraghi (d.1435) elaborated the technique further.

The writings of these important figures are difficult for musicians today to work with, as few are used to reading rhythmic values as numbers or poetic feet. Nonetheless, there has been at least one serious attempt to use them as a basis for making music. Lebanese researcher, violinist, and composer Nidaa Abu Mrad directed a collaborative project using notations of melodies by al-Urmawi, and one melody attributed to him but notated by Qutb al-Din, as a basis for a CD release (Ensemble de Musique Classique Arabe de l'Université Antonine 2005). His ensemble interpreted the notations using al-Urmawi's theorization of pitch and its relationship to frets of the oud at the time (al-Zalzal's fret mentioned in Chapter 10 in particular). They also played instruments known to have been in use in the thirteenth century: along with the oud, there is *qanun*, *riqq,* and *kamancheh*. All al-Urmawi's notations are very short, seeming to be skeletal extractions and leaving a great deal to the imagination. For the CD recording the musicians ornament them and—in line with al-Urmawi's indication—play them in various modes. Qutb al-Din's notation of

"*Ya Malikan*," in contrast, is full enough to be transcribed into a score and is played on the recording as an exceptional example of a song of the time.

After al-Urmawi and Qutb al-Din, the next and much more substantial source of music comes from the Ottoman court. This is a collection of notations by the musician-turned slave-turned interpreter Wojciech Bobowski (1610–1675). Bobowski was born in Bobowa (Poland) and worked initially as a church musician before being taken by the Ottomans, converting to Islam, and accepting the name Ali Ufki (Feldman 1996, 67ff). His "Collection of Instrumental and Vocal Works" (*Mecmua-i saz ü söz*) from the mid-1600s is notated in western staff notation, but from right to left to incorporate song texts. It contains several hundred pages of instrumental genres (*semai* and *pesrev*) and vocal pieces, spanning courtly, Sufi (Mevlevi), and popular styles. The pieces he recorded must have been the repertoire being played in the decades when he was working in Istanbul, from the 1630s to the 1650s.[9] One hundred of the instrumental pieces in Ali Ufki's collection also appear in another very substantial anthology, the treatise and collection (*Kitabu ilmi'l-musiki ala vechi'l-hurufat*) of Demetrius Cantemir (1673–1723), a Moldavian prince known in Turkey as Kantemiroglu (Feldman 1996, 30ff). Whereas Ali Ufki wrote his collection

for himself, Kantemiroglu was commissioned by two officials in the treasury to write his, and it is shaped by his theoretical concerns—the treatise is a major study of *makam* (the Turkish spelling for the Arabic *maqam*) and an exploration of the importance of notation. The 352 pieces he included are likely his transcriptions of music he knew by ear and are exclusively instrumental pieces of the court (Wright 1992b)[10]. The formal and stylistic range suggests that they included contemporary pieces—including his own compositions—and older ones. Kantemiroglu used an alphabetic system, rather than staff notation, just as did some musicians of the Mevlevi order of Sufism in the same period. He used the name of the note to choose the letter with which to identify it and added a number to specify its duration. The music was not composed for any specific instrument, but we know that the oud was one of the central instruments at the court until the early 1600s and was likely played elsewhere in the city for much longer.

These Ottoman anthologies not only present us with a large repertoire of music that can be played on the oud, they also allow us to imagine a little about the culture of music making. Most obviously, the names of the composers reveal the mixing of regional traditions at the court. Kantemiroglu does not name the composers of most pieces that seem stylistically the oldest, categorizing them as *acemler* and *hindi*, terms that referred to Persians and Indians. The court had modeled its cultural life on the Persianate Timurid Empire's capital of Herat at the turn of the fifteenth century, and Persian musicians were crucial to its development. Although the Persians are not named, several named composers in Kantemiroglu's collection were not Turkish or Muslim: Angeli was Greek, Härün Yahudi was Jewish, and there was at least one Armenian, Murad Çelebi.

It seems it was unusual for oud players (or any other instrumentalists) to be composers (Feldman 1996, 47), except in the case of members of Sufi orders, aristocrats, and royalty. In the ensuing centuries, the divide between vocalist-composers on the one hand and instrumentalists on the other, widened in the Ottoman court. Just as we have seen in the Abbasid court, slave women were crucial to court entertainment. Numerous male musicians were enslaved as well, and their names have rarely been preserved. (Oud player Mir Mehemmed, captured in Baghdad in 1638, is one exception.) It may be their captive status that led compositions by Persian musicians to be grouped together under the title *acemler*, rather than recognized with individual names.

This Iranian-Turkish repertoire has been recorded in varying styles by contemporary musicians. On the Turkish side, the historical oud reconstructions by Turkish luthier Saçit Gürel shape the resonance of a CD recording of some of Kantemiroglu's notations (*In Search of the Lost Sound* by Bezmara (2000)). This disc includes *pesrev*s from the *acemler* category, and some by the Crimean ruler Gazi II Giray (1554–1607), a prolific contemporary composer. There are also pieces by the composer named Angeli, by another referred to as Dervish Mustafa, and by Kantemiroglu himself. On the Iranian side, Arash Mohafez published not only a double CD collection of the *acemler,* titled *Ajamlar*, but also a new score of these pieces, including a scholarly commentary (Mohafez 2013; 2015).

These reconstructions of sound from historical notation bridge the period between 1600 and the present day. Where once the sound of Istanbul flowed into text, in Istanbul and Tehran, now the text has been translated into modern notation and then realized again in sound. These reconstruction processes are part of the transformation of music triggered by industrial recording in the twentieth century. Recordings today are understood as documents of research and "re-sounding" of the past, but they have also changed what it is to make music "in the here and now." Nowhere is this clearer than in the practice of *taksim* and the cultures of oud playing that we will explore next.

29. PRELUDING, EXPLORATION, COMPOSITION

Taksim (*taqasim, taqsim*) is the name given in Turkish and Arabic to an individual performer's more-or-less improvised, non-metrical creation of a modal melody. Our earliest traces of its existence with this name date from the late-sixteenth-century Ottoman Empire, a time of intense development and the professionalization of court music (Feldman 1996, 275–85). However, the Persian form of *taksim* (today referred to as *avaz*) had likely been in existence for some time, because it was known in the seventeenth-century Ottoman capital. This is clear from Kantemiroglu's comments. *Taksim* was distinct from composed genres of the time for several reasons, most fundamentally because it was unmeasured, not subject to the rhythmic cycles that were otherwise so fundamental to music. It seems initially to have been a vocal practice, which instrumentalists then took up, and it is therefore likely that the prosodic style emerges from Qur'anic recitation, *tajwid*. During the nineteenth century, vocal *taksim* gained its own distinct name, *gazel*. Today there are numerous other forms of unmeasured musical development in the region outside the elite court hubs, and there may well have been at the time as well.

A central feature of the *taksim* since the seventeenth century has been its on-the-spot creation. But at the court, at least, its function was nevertheless to allow musicians to present and elaborate the established "path," or *seyir,* of a *makam*. This meant that *taksim* was a vehicle not for the player's free expression, but for the demonstration of a player's grasp of *makam* and their ability to modulate through the various possible phases of its codified development. The Persian system was much more formulaic, based on a system of melodic fragments (*gushe*s) that had to be memorized and then reproduced in a specific order. However, these fragments required a lot of ornamentation and elaborations that would have been out of place in the Ottoman style. In both cases, a substantial amount of preparation lay behind the apparently spontaneous creation.

Fig. 64. One of the earliest writers on taksim, Dimitrie Cantemir (Kantemiroglu), commemorated on a postage stamp in Moldova, where he served as military commander in 1693 and 1710–1711.

While the Persian and Ottoman contexts created the antecedents for what has been standardized today, *taksim*-making was still a community activity. In the latter part of the seventeenth century, Ottoman performers gradually built on the Persian foundations to create some new styles of presentation. One of these was the *fasil*, or concert suite, which generally involved a group of instrumentalists and at least one singer (Feldman 1996, 182–83). An instrumental *taksim* served to introduce the pieces; then after two instrumental compositions (*pesrevs*) there was a vocal *taksim* with the *ney* and *tanbur* players accompanying; there were then some vocal genres (*beste*, also Persian *naks* and *kar*) and more instrumental pieces before a vocal *taksim* concluded the event (again, with instrumentalists accompanying). By the late eighteenth century, the Persian genres had been removed (as had the oud). There were also instrumental *fasils* by then, which placed increasing importance on the *taksim*, so much so that it became the core element, surrounded by instrumental pieces.

A kind of preluding and improvisation of interludes seems to have been a standard aspect of oud playing in Abbasid times, when the capacity to produce a melody to order was such a key skill. However, it seems to have been Ottoman influence on the Arab world that led the more developed, modern *taksim* to have real importance in the popular genre of suite (*wasla*) in Egypt and Syria. Ottoman influence also seems to have led players to embrace—at least in part—the idea of following the *seyir* of a *makam*. The Arab world gradually absorbed Ottoman court genres as well; Egyptians composed *semais* and *pesrevs* (the Arabic term for the latter is *bashraf*) during the nineteenth century as well.

The recording industry transformed the styles of development, and lengths of the *taksims* in the region were transformed fundamentally for several reasons. First, 78 rpm vinyl recordings could contain only three minutes of continuous music, so *taksims* conformed more or less to this length when they were recorded from the 1920s onward. Second, as players were recorded playing these short *taksims*, the recordings became a separate genre, and with it an individualistic solo culture emerged. This has stayed with us today. As technology has gradually allowed for more sustained production, oud players have come to record more extended pieces as *taksims*, or "improvisations," as they have been termed by many from outside the region where they originally developed.

The extent to which these are truly spontaneous creations or improvisations is questionable. The recording process, and the increasing professionalization of concert life, has made reliability and predictability important. Comparison between *taqsim* recordings by the iconic player Farid al-Atrash (1910–1974), for example, reveals a large degree of uniformity. Certain recordings have achieved celebrated status, such as the *taqsim*s of Egyptian oud player Muhammad al-Qasabji (1892–1966) and the six *taqsim*s of Egyptian Riyad al-Sunbati (1906–1981), and students are encouraged to imitate them as part of the learning process. Today one of the main "badges" of playing the oud is the ability to sit alone and create a *taqsim*, so these models are extremely helpful, particularly when people seek to learn oud while living in places where it is not played. These days a degree of structural planning— even notation—is encouraged and practiced by many players. If a player needs to deliver a *taksim* in the recording studio (where time is expensive), it will be very carefully prepared. And it will be naturally reproducible in concert. In other words, it will be a composition, even if subject to elaboration.

Muhammad al-Qasabji: Taqasim Rast

Fig. 65. An oud owned by Muhammad al-Qasabji (unknown maker). Private collection.

From the early era of phonograph recordings, the number of surviving oud *taksim*s is small in the context of other music, but many of them are taken as models for what oud playing "is." The historical *taksim*s of players from Istanbul who recorded in the 1920s, such Nevres Bey (1873–1937) and Yorgo Bacanos (1900–1977), have been transcribed and analyzed in detail. The same is true of the Iraqi Azuri Haruni's *taksim*s and Tunisian Khemais Tarnan's *istikhbar*s (*istikhbar* is a North African practice similar to *taksim*) recorded at the Cairo Congress of 1932 (Verrier 2015). There are fascinating qualities in these recordings, and they are reference points for many players today. But taking them as our principal models risks leading us to imagine the oud as a vehicle for individual reflections by men! We will explore counternarratives in Chapter 32.

In fact those now iconic *taksim* recordings should be recognized both as outgrowths of Islamic and Ottoman court culture and as part of the European influence on cultural practices regionally, particularly the interest in recording. The choices of the recording industry were driven initially by European market concerns, and they contributed to the focus on solo artistry. The violin had become a leading player in Egyptian ensembles by the late nineteenth century (another European influence), and players recorded solo *taksim*s on violin, just as they did on *qanun* and *ney*. In 1920s Istanbul, Turkish singer Münir Nurettin Selçuk (1899–1981) came to represent "the soloist," as part of a broad cultural turn toward western practices considered progressive and modern (O'Connell 2016). We return to the emergence of the soloist in Chapter 31, but first we will look at another development.

Yorgo Bacanos: Huseyni Taksim

Fig. 66. Yorgo Bacanos with his brother Aleko.
Photo by Mustafa Karatas.

30. CANONICAL REPERTOIRES

Europeans were fascinated by the spontaneous musical creation of *taksim* throughout the twentieth century, and numerous oud players and other instrumentalists found ways to benefit, as we will see in Part VII. However, over the same period there was a growing trend in the opposite direction, toward consolidation of notated repertories understood as "canonical" or "classical." The formation of canons and classical traditions is associated with the elite classes, but also with national values and national cultures. Unsurprisingly, national movements engendered several notated corpora in the Middle East. These reflect a kind of "becoming like Europe" in order to be understood as on a par with Europe. They often were inspired by movements toward national independence, but they were equally often partially sponsored by European colonial governments.

A striking example is how the repertoire known as *maluf* in Tunisia, which is a heterogeneous body of repertoire including multiple genres from multiple neighboring regions (*nuba, qasida, shughul, bashraf, istikhbar, zendeli, muwashshah,* and *zajal*). In the nineteenth and early twentieth centuries, *maluf* was used to refer to the music of Sufi ceremonies, where it was enjoyed by men singing in chorus and clapping (sometimes with a percussion instrument) (Davis 2004). In some urban centers *maluf* was also played in secular spaces with a small ensemble of melodic instruments as well, including the

oud arbi—the four-course oud (as described in Chapter 23 above) that was played in varying but similar tunings throughout the Maghreb. Today *maluf* has acquired a particular status as the core of the national classical repertoire and crucial to the study of the *oud arbi*, and Tunisian music generally.

Maluf became a national repertoire in part due to Tunisian independence in 1956. It was also a consequence of the earlier collaboration between Tunisian musician and literary scholar Shaykh Ahmad al-Wafi (d. 1921) and Baron Rodolphe d'Erlanger (1872–1932), a French-born researcher, along with musicians such as oud player Khemais Tarnan. D'Erlanger's five-volume study, *La musique arabe,* and his patronage and fostering of music in his palace in Sidi Bou Said in Tunisia, helped lay the ground for the subsequent developments (Davis 2002; 1992). There had already been some work undertaken in notating traditional music, notably a manuscript from the military school of Bardo from 1872 (Morra 2018, 52). However, d'Erlanger argued that Tunisian musical heritage was endangered because of its lack of a theoretical system and one of notation. He contributed to the conception and planning of a major festival and symposium on Arab music, which ultimately took place in Cairo in 1932 with the support of the Egyptian government. This now famous Congress of Arab Music brought together the

Europeans Béla Bartók and Robert Lachmann, along with musicians from numerous countries of West Asia, and it continues to benefit us today with its remarkable recorded archive, along with numerous documents (Ali Jihad Racy 1991).

D'Erlanger's efforts to promote the study of modern Arab music theory and notation outlived him. Two years after his death, the Tunisian state subsidized the establishment of the Rashidia Institute dedicated to the preservation and promotion of Tunisian music. Violinist Muhammad Triki (with training in European, Middle Eastern, and Tunisian music) was employed to create notations of repertoire known to players invited to play in the institute's ensemble. No less than five oud players came forward to volunteer repertoire for the collection and play, which presented a challenge for notation as they all played slightly different versions. In consequence Triki requested that the various shaykhs agree on a version of melodies they knew, and he would then notate it. This melodic standardization resulted in nine volumes of notated music published in 1956, *al-Turath al-musiqi al-tunisi* (The Traditional Music of Tunisia), which was distributed among Rashidia Institutes around the country (Davis 1992).

The most celebrated player of this period was Tarnan, who was also one of the founders of the Rashidia Institute. His name is associated strongly with the era, not least because of his institutional role,

his recordings at the Cairo Congress, and his recordings for commercial labels. He was not actually the only oud player, and in the large Rashidia ensemble there were sometimes as many as six. But Tarnan developed a broad representative function as well; in the 1960s, he and his *oud arbi* appeared on Tunisian postage stamps, cementing the link between the nation and the instrument, and by implication, *maluf*. By that time, the *maluf* was on the way to becoming associated exclusively with the Rashidia Institute and—perhaps because of that—was played very little in informal secular settings for some decades. The Tunisian *oud arbi* remains closely associated with ideas about the Tunisian nation, even while it is also associated with the broader idea of the Andalusian legacy and—especially since 2011—has been played in more diverse locations, including informal clubs (Morra 2018, 62–67).

The process of standardizing widely known but varied repertoires happened in a rather different way in Iran, but there are distinct similarities. Once again there was a key figure who took European principles as a model through which to modernize local music education, while undertaking theoretical study and promoting notation for traditional music. This time, it was Ali Naghi Vaziri (1886–1979), the first Iranian to study music in Europe, who also became Professor of Aesthetics at the University of Tehran (Farhat 2004, 8–9). Like in the Tunisian case, the notation of a core repertoire was important, which in Iran was termed *radif*, which means "row" or "series" (Nettl 1992). Somewhat like Tunisia, in Iran several distinguished musicians' repertoires served as the foundation, but rather than being unified into one, these were laid down in many different versions, each representing the selection of a particular musician and his teaching material. Each *radif* therefore reflects the musician whose *radif* it is, whether it is for instrument or voice. There are the *radif*s of Mirza Abdollah (1843–1918) for *tar* and *setar*, for example, and *radif*s by Abolhasan Saba (1902–1957) for *santur*, violin, *setar*, and *tar*, which are organized modally but also function like instruction books for each instrument. Vocal *radif*s incorporate poetry, such as those by singers Abdollah Davami (1891–1980) and Mahmoud Karimi (b.1968). Today these and similar collections form the core study material for any instrumentalist or singer, and more conservative musicians in the Iranian classical tradition would insist that without being able to demonstrate at least one entire *radif*, one is not a mature musician. But the most important distinction from the Tunisian case is that whereas the oud was a strong member of the ensemble at the time of the standardization in Tunisia, the oud was still very much neglected in Iran—as it had been for centuries.

This situation has changed gradually since the 1970s, primarily as a result of efforts by musician Iskandar Ibrahimi (1935–2015). He commissioned luthier Nariman Abnoosi to make him an oud (Beckles Willson and Bouban 2018). Abnoosi based his measurements on an instrument that had come into Iran from Iraq. When he became an oud player Ibrahimi adopted the first name of the luthier Nariman Abnoosi and called himself Mansur Nariman. He began teaching oud at the Conservatory of Tehran; he created a *radif* for oud, along with a method book and a collection of compositions.

Rachel Beckles Willson playing Nariman's "Shurangiz", composed for oud

Fig. 67. Rachel Beckles Willson.

However, the oud was associated strongly with the Arab world and had not been part of the institutionalization processes of the preceding decades. So it was not until 1994 that Nariman was able to get it accepted as a major, or principal study, and Iranian repertoires and aesthetics remain dominated by a core of other instruments. Despite its ancient Sassanian history, it is therefore "young" in Iran today, and Iranian oud players have to work hard to adapt the standard repertoire, to make it convincingly playable on the oud. One of the most significant contributors to this project is Negar Bouban, who developed a strong profile as a soloist through her own adaptations and developments of established genres such as the *chaharmezrab*. Bouban has also contributed substantially to pedagogical innovation, and her publications and teaching practice strive for a different kind of "modernization" from the one instigated by Vaziri. As she has said in an interview:

> It's my own idea of putting materials into a lesson-like arrangement that's more task-based rather than just presenting or doing things on the instrument, which in my opinion is mostly based on imitation. I intend to have different aspects of the music involved and achieve more in a balance. Often I find teachings kind of off-balance—they mostly rely on repeating things, imitating a thousand times, after which maybe you get half of it or less. I hate this, I think it's boring, it takes a lot of energy, and it's not efficient. (Beckles Willson and Bouban 2018)

Bouban's remarks hint at the real tension between the creation of a standard repertoire and the creative practicing musician. When a canon is formed it tends to be followed by an entrenchment of norms and hierarchies, along with rather oppressive orthodoxies that play out in social as well as musical spheres. And yet it can provide a rich basis—a sort of "language" of phrases and modal relations—that can be explored, combined, and adjusted to make new repertoires. In their ways, all oud-playing cultures are exploring this process, as they have done for centuries.

Negar Bouban playing Hossein Alizadeh's Chaharmezrab Abu Atar arranged for oud

31. THE SOLO REPERTOIRE

As we gathered from sources on the Abbasid era in Chapter 15, the oud was used for solo display in the distant past, even while its main role has probably always been the support of the human voice. What happened in the twentieth century was a dramatic increase in solo activity. This was on the increase when the Arab prince Sherif Muhiddin Haydar, also known as Sherif Muhiddin Targan, was growing up in Istanbul and studying classical Ottoman music with the oud. Sherif Muhidin was also studying cello, and in time he would take his instruments with him to New York, where he attempted to build a career as a musician. This experience—he was privileged enough to mingle with luminary virtuosi on the western classical scene—encouraged him to break away from the generic compositional work he had been doing (such as composing *semais*) and start composing solo music for the oud that resembled showpieces for violin or cello.

The radical nature of what he did was not just his import of arpeggio figuration, fast scales, and use of the extreme upper register. It was also the way that he set aside traditional *makam* development in melody, which tends toward a gradual unfolding and extension of range, with recurrences of reference notes. He also set aside the forms provided by the classical genres of *pesrev* and *semai*. *Caprice* (1923), for example, is a slightly rhapsodic collection of dramatic gestures, such as rapidly repeating chords, fast scales, and what Julian Harris calls "hopping melodies" on one string (Harris 2018, 91). In other pieces, he used a hint of what in European traditions is called "programmatic" music—pieces expressing particular sentiments or illustrating a character, what in European traditions might be called "character pieces." This was new to oud playing, while it was rather old-fashioned in western classical composition.

Sherif Muhiddin Targan: "Caprice"

Fig. 68. Sherif Muhiddin Targan.

Fig. 69. *Sherif Muhiddin Targan: vinyl record made in New York, 1925.*

Sherif Muhiddin did not receive substantial interest in his innovations in Istanbul, although his approach was admired by the singer Münir Nurettin Selçuk mentioned above. Neither the model of oud virtuoso nor the format of solo recital took off in the city, so it is difficult to know what impact he would have had, had he not been invited to Baghdad to direct the music department of the newly established Institute for Fine Arts. The Cairo Congress of Arabic Music had led to a dissemination of the idea that the future of regional music depended on the adaptation of European principles of music education for *makam* (*maqam* in Arabic) traditions. Sherif Muhiddin worked alongside the Iraqi Hanna Butrus (b. 1896) and strove to increase Iraqi awareness of western classical music, while he also developed a distinct style of oud pedagogy. The oud tutorial he published is a dense collection of technical exercises, including his adaptation of some cello techniques (Targan 1995).

Among his first class of students, the one who extended this virtuosic style most intensively was the prodigiously talented oud player and violinist Jamil Bashir (1921–1977), already mentioned in Chapter 10. Born in Mosul to Iraqi Assyrian parents, Jamil started learning oud from his father, a singer and a well-known oud player, at around the age of six. His talent led the family to move to Baghdad in 1937, where he studied at the Institute of Fine Arts and gradually established a position of immense authority. Already Inspector of Music in schools, and Director of Music on the radio, when Sherif Muhiddin left Baghdad in 1948, Jamil succeeded him as Director of Music at the Institute of Fine Arts. At that point, his younger brother, Munir, was eighteen, and both the talent and exuberant personality of Jamil may have kept Munir in the shade for some time. However, as we will explore in Chapter 38, Munir's moment was to come.

We can trace Jamil's virtuosity in his compositions, but also in the way he formalized and systematized the extended use of the oud in a method and repertoire book (J. Bashir 1961b). Published in 1961 and made obligatory in music schools by the Ministry of Education, it surely benefitted from his many years of work in education. He taught both oud and violin at the Institute of Fine Arts, where his many students included Atika al-Khazraji, a renowned poet and lecturer at Baghdad University. The oud method also benefited from his study of western methods while learning violin; his violin playing is a little-explored but remarkable area of his musicianship.

According to Jean-Claude Chabrier, an early commentator, Bashir's students lamented the fact that he did not advance his performing career in Europe in the 1960s. But early in that decade, he suffered cardiac problems that necessitated a step back even from his work at the Institute for Fine Arts. Some of the flamboyance of his attitude can be traced in a challenge to virtuosi that he created two years before he died. The Lebanese magazine *Achabaka* published his "Samai Nahawand," stating that whoever could play it would win a substantial prize. Nobody volunteered, so the prize went unclaimed. It provides another example of how authority was increasingly determined by notated music, and the capacity to place oneself under its rule.

Raed Kosahaba playing Jamil Bashir's Samai Nahawand

Fig. 70. *"Samai Nahawand" by Jamil Bashir. Reproduced from Achabaka, 13 Jan 1975.*

While Sherif Muhiddin's compositions are divided between Ottoman genres and European-style showpieces, Bashir's piece combined the traditional Ottoman *semai* with extravagantly virtuosic figuration and some melodies that seem to stretch the rhythmic pulse traditionally underpinning the genre. This approach, extending classical Ottoman genres, did not develop much further outside Turkey, presumably because the original repertoire was planted less deeply outside Istanbul. However, celebrated Turkish oud player and composer Yurdal Tokcan, building on his study of historical repertoires, has composed several *semai*s that are also quite elaborate showpieces and, in some cases, mood or character pieces as well. In Tokcan's *semai*s the underlying pulse remains important—part of the challenge is in making sure the very intricate figuration is smoothly contained within that.

Just as did Bashir, Tokcan has also contributed to the development of character pieces such as "Gürcü kizi" (Georgian girl), along with meditative pieces that show off his lusciously melodic, resonant style while exploring individual emotional states such as "Hislenis" (Deep emotion).

Yurdal Tokcan: "Hisleniş"

Fig. 71. Yurdal Tokcan.

Tokcan's stylistic contribution is particularly striking for this melodic development of the oud, which recalls the smooth, very vocal playing of Turkish oud player and singer Cinuçen Tanrıkorur (1938–2000). Tanrıkorur's preferred activity was singing with the oud, and he considered his own work to perpetuate the otherwise lost traditions of the *asik* (minstrels), but he too composed several innovative instrumental pieces based on classical genres, notably a *semai* called "Koyde Sabah" (Morning in the Village). Turkey has not supported a culture of solo performance, and while Tokcan's capacity as a virtuoso soloist is undeniable, he has developed his career mainly through ensemble work, whether with the Turkish State Ensemble or smaller groups.

Cinuçen Tanrıkorur: Tarla Dönüşü (also known as "Koyde Saba")

Today, the players who most value the solo oud hark from the sphere of influence that developed in Baghdad at the time of Sherif Muhiddin, spreading through his first group of students including Jamil Bashir, Salman Shukur (1920–2007), and Ghanim Haddad (1925–2012), and the many others who trained and worked in Baghdad a little later, such as Jamil's younger brother, Munir Bashir (1930–1997), Rahim AlHaj (b.1968), Ehsen El Emam, and Raed Koshaba. They tend to be collectively referred to as being part of an "Iraqi school," while not one of them has actually been able to live in Iraq in recent decades. Now living variously in the Gulf, Egypt, Europe, and North America, several of them teach the principles of methodical technical training established in Baghdad by Sherif Muhiddin and Jamil Bashir.

Fig. 72. Cinucen Tanrıkorur.

One of them—Naseer Shamma—founded a school in 1998, Bait Al Oud in Cairo, which subsequently opened a branch in the UAE. Bait Al Oud also cultivates the world of the soloist. It is therefore sharply distinct from the institutions discussed above in Tunisia and Iran, where emphasis is on a core repertoire and on studying an instrument in order to be able to play and extend that. At Bait Al Oud the curriculum focuses primarily on individual instrumental technique and solfège (basic pitch recognition) while historical repertoire is comparatively sidelined, as is the challenge of working in ensembles. Where Sherif Muhiddin's work was enriched by his Ottoman background, and Jamil Bashir's work grew out of his work in traditional music in the region (and his study of European violin), not all players studying at the Bait Al Oud have such rich backgrounds or professional practices. Is there is a risk here that oud playing gets defined as a mechanical rather than a social and creative process?

What about the listening skills needed for ensemble playing, and the interactive skills that emerge from studying those? At Bait Al Oud there are ensembles, but they tend to be huge gatherings of oud students amassed on the stage to play in unison, each having learned the same text in the same way and each reproducing it in line with everyone else. Finally, what has happened here to the power of the oud as a support of the human voice, which has been a fundamental force in all music of the region?

In Abbasid times, it seems to have been common for large groups of oud players to play together, although they were most frequently women enslaved by the court or by other rich patrons. But these women also sang; oud playing in such cases was chorus-like and took place in accompaniment of group singing. There is a further difference today, which is that the amassed groups seem to be essentially part of a physical training and endurance program rather than viable forms of entertainment. Even if the players are not enslaved in the way they were at the time of the Abbasid court, they may seem uncannily army-like.

What repertoire is cultivated by oud players emerging from this cultural space? A range of answers can be found in the repertoire of oud soloists at the Global Oud Forum, which took place online at the 2021 Abu Dhabi Festival. Iraqi Yousif Abbas presented his own "Caprice in Makam Nahawand"—a showpiece building on the foundation of caprices by Sherif Muhiddin and Jamil Bashir (each of which were presented by other players). Several players presented compositions by Naseer Shamma, while Egyptian players such as Mohamed Abozekry, Hazem Shaheen, and Sherine Tohamy played their own compositions. Other oud traditions were drawn into the festival as well. There was a performance of the first movement of Beethoven's Fifth Symphony by Faisal al-Saari of UAE, for instance, continuing the trend of adapting western classical works for oud in which Farid al-Atrash was foundational. Farid's film *Min Agl Hubbi*, in which he plays the role of a professional musician, includes a concert performance of an arrangement for oud and orchestra of Spanish composer Albeniz's piece "Asturias" from his Suite Española no.1. Iraqi musician Salem Abdul Karim continued the practice, arranging works such as Vittorio Monti's *Csárdás* and Rimsky-Korsakov's *Flight of the Bumblebee*. Slightly differently, at the Global Oud Forum the Libyan Hisham Errish presented two compositions with references to European virtuosity in the titles ("To Paganini" and "To Chopin"), and this led him to explore new textures on the oud.

Equally striking was the resistance to these explicitly European virtuosic directions. Turkish player Necati Çelik presented two works from the classical Ottoman canon, while the Malaysian Zulkarnain Yusof played an elaboration of two "Malaysian-Arab" folk songs with accompanying instrumental tracks. The Sudanese Ashraf Awad's melodic compositions "Companionship" and "Seereh" are characterized most strongly by the mode associated with Africa traditions, pentatony.

The early-twentieth-century development of the recording industry has been transformed by changes in media from vinyl to tape to CD and back to vinyl—but most of all by the internet. Thanks to the internet, it was possible for the Abu Dhabi Festival to take place in 2021, despite a global pandemic, and to showcase oud players from both Europe and Asia. Playing as a soloist suddenly had a different meaning: it was less risky than playing in an ensemble. COVID-19 has propelled us into accepting and appreciating new norms, as even these reduced types of musical presentation allow us some sense of connection in a desperate time.

32. BEYOND THE PRINTED CANONS

While elite spaces have been very important to the history of the oud, offering one reason it is known as the "king" or "sultan" of instruments, a great deal of oud repertoire has grown up around the edges of privilege. Almost no trace of this activity survives in many cases—certainly no music notation—making it harder to write a history. But there are recollections passed on through generations; there are a few photos, and there are the partial, but helpful, remains of the early recording industry. These lead historians to ask themselves whether the apparent disappearance of the oud from the Ottoman court (as discussed in Chapter 19), misleads us, as we try to imagine the broader sphere of music-making. Could it be, some have asked, that the oud was nevertheless played consistently in homes, in clubs, and on the street, in a range of locations under Ottoman rule?

In the late era of empire, the answer is certainly affirmative in many urban spaces; the oud was played in popular music genres in numerous towns from Smyrna (today's Izmir) to Cairo and beyond. Most often it had a role in small ensembles and in accompanying singers, such as in the Egyptian ensemble *takht*, which comprised about five male musicians. As a musical formation, *takht* was admired and was distinguished by its celebrated singers such as Abdu al-Hamuli (1841(?)–1902) and

Shaykh Yusuf al-Manyalawi (1847–1911). The *takht* repertoire included music known to the musicians and passed down by ear, but it was also a vehicle for new work by composers such as Muḥammad Uthman (1855–1900). Like al-Hamuli, Uthman is strongly associated with the so-called revival of Arab music in this era. His *takht* (with oud player Ahmad al-Laythi) presented elaborate vocal genres of *muwashshah* and *dawr*, interspersed with some lighter songs and short instrumental pieces. Al-Hamuli had been taken to the Ottoman court by the Egyptian Khedive Ismail Pasha and was then able to bring back examples of the repertoire of Istanbul. Some *takht*s no doubt also played weighty instrumental genres drawn from Sufi and court circles, such as the *semai* and *bashraf* (*pesrev* in the Turkish sphere).

Women were on the edges of or were excluded from the *takht* formation, for the social reasons we explored in Section III. Courtly culture had shaped performance settings of Arab cities in this respect and in the predominance of private gatherings of male patrons. These closed circles spilled outward to the public mainly in festivities such as weddings. During the nineteenth century, there was also a spread of "coffee houses" (*qahawi*) in poorer areas of Cairo and an attendant anxiety about propriety, because women were present as singers and dancers in cafes and also as alcohol-selling staff. Some *takht* musicians avoided playing in such spaces, fearing for their own reputations. The presence of Europeans influenced the formation of nightclubs (variously termed *masraḥ, kazinu,* and *sala*), which brought greater opportunities for some women to organize events and perform more "respectably"—even if this meant to female audiences only.

In late Ottoman Smyrna and Salonika (Thessaloniki), the settings for small ensembles were often the drinking and hashish bars of the impoverished underclass, where communities were mixed in gender and ethnicity, including Arabs, Armenians, Jews, Romani, and Turks (Tragaki 2009, 11–12). (For the background to such mixed communities in Thessaloniki, see Chapter 33 below.) It is likely that the listeners came from a range of social strata and linguistic groups and were also familiar with the French-style cabaret venues in the same cities, *café-chantants*. They included students and intellectuals, family men and workers, visitors and travelers, and even Orthodox church cantors. The latter took a role indeed in evaluating vocal styles, and some participated themselves in secular music making. There was also an overlap with the world of Jewish chant. The Sephardic Jewish cantor Sadhik Gerson, who served at the Beth Israel Synagogue, also played oud and *santur*, and sang the secular genre *amanes* (Tragaki 2009, 287). The repertoire was therefore diverse, including Arab and Turkish tunes, Greek traditional songs, urban songs of port cities, and songs of ethnic groups that made up the mosaic of the region— Albanian, Bulgarian, Romani, Rumanian, and others. Their songs were linked by the modal and rhythmic world that underpinned the classical Ottoman repertoire as well, just as all sacred chant was embedded in the musical syntax of the eastern Mediterranean region.

The best-known of the oud players in this context is Hagop Stambulyan, an Armenian-Greek musician born in Istanbul (1891–1965). His recording career took off in Athens because he accompanied the rather successful Greek Jewish singer Roza Eskenazi (mid-1890s–1980); he took the Greek stage name Agapios Tomboulis. In the interwar years they recorded for Columbia and HMU, and toured Egypt, Albania, and Serbia. Today scholars use the term *rebetiko* for this repertoire associated with Athens; while for the branch of *rebetiko* involving the oud and the mixed communities of Asia Minor, the preferred expression is *Smyrneika*—in reference to Smyrna. There the main focus is on the singer and her/his reflections on the struggles of life, interrupted by long improvisatory passages sung to the syllables of the word "aman"—hence the name of the music bars where *Smyrneika* was

heard: *café-amans*. The oud player—and other instrumentalists on *kanun*, *santur*, or violin— offered introductory or intervening *taksim* as well as followed the vocal line.

Rosa Eshkenazi sings "My Sweet Canary", with oud introduction by Dimitris Tomboulis

Fig. 73. Lambros Leondaritis, Rosa Eshkenazi, Dimitris Tomboulis. Uncredited photo from vinyl recording Fünf Griechen in der Hölle (Tikont 1982).

The restrictions on female performers that were part of the Arab cultural sphere appeared in the Istanbul scene as well, where Muslim women were not allowed to record during the Ottoman Empire. The presence of female oud players in the early recording catalogs—Armenians, Jews, and Roma—suggests that the oud was played by women quite widely, whether or not they could do so commercially or be acknowledged. The female oud player Hayriye Örs evidently contributed significantly but is difficult to trace; there is a photo with an uncertain annotation, and Pathé recordings on which she is named, whereas on others there is an unnamed oud player, most likely her. In this respect, Hamiyet Yuceses (1915–1996) was born at a fortunate time, because when the Turkish Republic was established, restrictions for Muslim women were greatly reduced. Classically trained, Yuceses became a celebrated singer and oud player on the Turkish music hall scene.

One of the non-Muslim oud players was Victoria Hazan (1896–1995), who was born in Izmir to Jewish parents and who sang, played, and composed for Turkish and Jewish cultural circles before and after her emigration to America in 1920. Numerous other women were nightclub variety artists, and the majority were Armenian or Roma. Nezihe Hanim and Anjel Hanim (who also played the piano) feature in recollections of performances and in record catalogs, for instance; a third one, Vedia Rıza, seems not to have performed live but was active as a singer and oud player on the radio and then on record (Barutcu 2019).

Thanks to the research of Sonia Tamar Seeman, we know more about Nasip Hanim, a female Romani singer and oud player who had a lively career before she died in 1925 (date of birth unknown). Seeman has had to read between the lines of the biographies of others to find information about Nasip, whose talents and success was not in line with the prevailing discourse, in which Romani were presented as degraded and dangerous (Seeman 2021, 188–92). She was highly sought-after for private concerts in aristocratic circles, and her popularity is clear from her numerous recordings with prominent musicians of her time. Hers was reputedly the first female voice to be recorded in Istanbul. She played on many vocal records, composed at least one song, and probably recorded numerous instrumental pieces as well, in ensembles. One has survived, a *pesrev* by Tatyos Ekserciyan, recorded for Zonophone in 1904, with Armenian violinist Karekine and Greek Romani *kemençe* player Anastas. In their ensemble there is heterophony; the instrumentalists play different versions of the melody simultaneously (Seeman 2021, xxi). It gives us a taste of what Muhammad Triki confronted when he attempted to notate the *maluf* (Chapter 30) and also recalls the heterophony typical of the historical *takht* of the Arab world (A. J. Racy 2004, 80–82). This internal variation between

THE
OUD

160

players contrasts with the unison playing of ensembles such as those of Bait Al Oud.

What did the oud mean to the people who played it in this now bygone era? It is not impossible that it had a particular significance for young middle-class women, reminding us—rather surprisingly perhaps—of the significance of the lute in eighteenth-century England, when (according to Mary Burwell at least, as seen in Chapter 18) it was a vehicle for catching a husband. Numerous female oud players appear in Turkish literary works published 1874–1922,[10] and according to a nostalgic article published in Istanbul in 1950, well-to-do families all arranged for the daughters to learn oud. According to that writer, "not playing oud was simply regarded as a flaw in prospective brides" (Arınç, Moser, and Stokes 2017). Was oud playing a standard domestic pastime and entertainment for young women? The group of women portrayed in the postcard shown in figure 74a – surrounded by ruins – is suggestive of a lost, and partially recovered music culture, shortly after the collapse of the empire.

One further literary work provides an intriguing counterpoint, *Udi* by Fatma Aliye. Aliye based her novel on an oud player she met in Aleppo, Bedia, who suffered intensely from the patriarchy of the world around her. After she lost her father and divorced her unfaithful husband, her oud became her "most loyal and reliable friend." For Bedia,

the instrument was a consolation in solitary independence, rather than a vehicle for creating a bond with anyone else.

Figs. 74a and 74b. Postcard sent from Constaninople in 1929.
No copyright traced.

CHANGING OUD REPERTOIRES

161

Part VII

A MOSAIC OF MOVING OUD-PLAYING CULTURES FROM THE 20TH & 21ST CENTURIES

For centuries, the story of the oud was bound up with the story of empire, and particularly the Ottoman Empire. In this final section, we explore how the post-Ottoman world shapes the life of the oud: a century of movement and transformation of oud-playing cultures.

Fig. 75. Ahmad Al Khatib, an internationally distinguished oud player born in a Palestinian refugee camp in Jordan, now living in Sweden.

33.   REFUGEES WITH OUDS: THE EXAMPLES OF THESSALONIKI AND NEW YORK

The last decades of the Ottoman Empire were far from tranquil. Surrounding and competing empires—Russian, British, and French—made increasingly successful encroachments, and tension within the realm increased. The Armenian communities suffered the most. Under the Ottoman Empire, they had a subordinate but protected status but lost the protection during "reforms" of the nineteenth century. Their protests were met with accusations of being a threat to the pan-Islamic empire, an idea reinforced by their main religious affiliation (Christian) and in some regions also their wealth. There were massacres in the 1890s and in 1909, then in 1915 a program of Islamification, deportations, and concentration camp deaths culminating in the genocide by the Ottoman "Committee of Union and Progress." Many other Christian communities were killed at the same time.

Who knows how many musicians died, and how many were forced to uproot themselves and seek lives elsewhere. Those who left were ethnically and linguistically diverse, but they carried with them the shared sounds and expressions of Anatolia, and they spread them wide and far—throughout Greece and Lebanon, but also well beyond.

Thessaloniki's cosmopolitan hashish bar world, mentioned above in Chapter 30, had already been substantially transformed by refugees. By the end of World War I, the city and in particular its music were transformed further, as the 1923 population exchange between the newly consolidated Greek and Turkish Republics led refugees to make up one-third of Thessaloniki's population. They dominated the popular music scene with their repertoires and styles from Smyrna and Istanbul (Tragaki 2009, 53).

Thessaloniki saw numerous other changes in the 1920s, which brought opportunities and challenges for musicians. Hitherto the music scene had been shaped by the relationship between musicians and audiences, but increasingly the more important negotiations were between musicians and recording companies. It led to some standardization in repertoire and packaging to suit the market. A "professional ensemble" emerged, for instance, the *santouroviola*, which was based on *santur* and violin but often included oud (Tragaki 2009, 49).

Another development was more of a threat to the oud. There was fresh competition from the type of *rebetiko* associated with the port of Pireaus in Athens, where the bouzouki (fretted lute) was dominant, along with its equal-tempered tuning (Tragaki 2009, 65f.). Bouzouki-dominated *rebetiko* won ground because of much wider movements of post-Ottoman refugees and the intercontinental media channels that carried their music. Between 1916 and 1929, numerous people from Asia Minor traveled to and settled in North America, many of them joining the recently settled immigrant communities of New York, whether in Little Syria, Little Armenia, or the areas associated with Greeks or Sephardic and Romaniote Jews (Nagoski 2011). By the late 1920s, their recordings of *rebetiko* involving the bouzouki had some commercial success. They were associated with a straight, nasal style of vocal delivery characteristic of traditional Greek song (very distinct from the florid *amanes*). Musicians in Greece were encouraged to cater to the same market and record with the bouzouki, also with the *baghlamas* (a small bouzouki) and guitar. Their recordings became increasingly popular in the 1930s, pushing musicians from Istanbul and Smyrna into the shade. As a result, the oud fell out of fashion.

Over time, long-standing debates about "oriental" music and its social worlds emerged again and fed into heated media discussions about the propriety of the *rebetiko* scene, until the Greek dictator Metaxas placed a ban on all *rebetiko* activity in 1936. In practice, the ban was not completely effective. Nevertheless, the 1930s witnessed the gradual erosion and near demise of the culture of melismatic *amanes*, *makams* with inflected tuning patterns, and the oud playing that supported them.

While the commercial success of records arriving from North America contributed to the decline of the oud in Greek cities, it is not the case that all émigré musicians neglected the oud. Thanks to archived and rereleased recordings from the 1920s, we can get a tantalizing sense of some players, even while very little is known about them (Nagoski 2011). Who was Arap Neset Bey, who died in 1930 leaving a collection of *oud taksim* recordings published by HMU and Odeon? Presumably he was an Arabic speaker, whereas others of whom we know little were part of the Armenian community. M. Douzjian, who recorded songs for M. G. Parsekkian and Pharos, was probably Mugirdich Douzjian, born in 1896 and who arrived in America in 1921 and settled in Union City, New Jersey. Karekin Proodian (b. 1884) arrived at the age of ten from the Black Sea coast and joined his father in Worcester, Massachusetts, going on to record in both Armenian and Turkish, and founding his own label. He also recorded with Assyrian singer Kosroff Malool (b. ca. 1881), the first to release a Kurdish song in America. One of the most celebrated oud player-singers was the Greek Achilleas Poulos (b. 1893), who recorded over 100 performances in the 1920s.

Life could not have been easy for this generation of oud-playing immigrants, even in the bustling 1920s. Suffering from arthritis, Achilleas Poulos stopped recording in 1927. He and his wife ran two Manhattan cafes that were popular with immigrants (and that served alcohol despite prohibition), but these, as so much else, came to an abrupt halt in the economic crisis of 1929. The most popular immigrant singer, Marika Papagika, and her husband, Costas, opened a Manhattan club in 1925, but it lasted only a few years for the same reason. Repertoire that captured the imagination of Americans—and thus brought immigrant musicians commercial success—had no need for oud. The "oriental" oboe melody of Tetos Dimitriadis's song "Misirlou," released in 1927, was probably more appealing. It was certainly covered by many American musicians and bands over ensuing decades.

34. JERUSALEM JUNCTION

The struggles around migrating ouds and oud players take many forms, particularly when they become the focus for diverging world views. Palestinian chronicler, oud player, and singer Wasif Jawharriyeh (1897–1972) narrated a conflict he had with a Jewish refugee from Germany, whose thinking was shaped by (and had contributed to) contemporary European ethnomusicology. Fascinated by the diversity of music he heard in in Jerusalem, this Robert Lachmann (1892–1939) interviewed and recorded Jawharriyeh (among many other musicians) and invited him to illustrate at least one of his lectures on Arab music. Jawharriyeh took the opportunity to challenge Lachmann about his views publicly. While Lachmann argued that Arab music should be learned in the traditional way that Jawharriyeh himself had enjoyed— by listening to and imitating a teacher in one-on-one lessons, learning melodies phrase by phrase—Jawharriyeh argued that Arab music would be held back if musicians could not benefit from methods based on notation. Only a few individuals could access one-on-one lessons, he said, and the tradition could not develop with such small numbers (Beckles Willson 2014, XV).

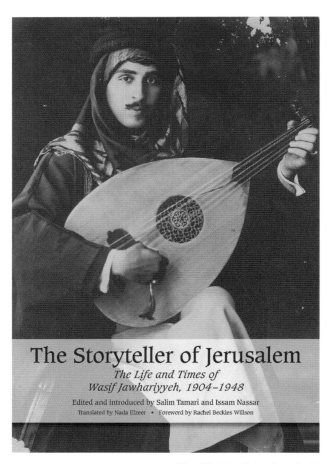

Fig. 76. Wasif Jawharriyeh.

As we saw in Chapter 28 above, in the cases of Tunisia and Iran, there was considerable regional interest in transforming repertories into notation and developing new styles of teaching based on them (also in Iraq, see Chapter 31). Jawharriyeh's own reference point was Egypt, whose musicians he had followed with admiration since childhood. As he explained to Lachmann, musicians studying European staff notation and theory in Egypt had been stimulated, rather than restricted, by it. He pointed to the examples of oud player and composer Abd al-Wahhab and the large orchestra accompanying singer Umm Kulthum. His argument was not only music-theoretical; it was also political, because staff notation had become the main technology for the study of music and for gaining access to the music profession. Without understanding and using staff notation, he said, Arab musicians would not be able to develop their traditions for the modern world. (At the time of writing his recollections, Jawharriyeh may or may not have known the sad tale of Muhammad Abd al-Karim, the Syrian *buzuq* player at the Palestine Broadcasting Service who refused to learn notation and was fired by controller Ajaj Nuwayhid in 1940 (Beckles Willson 2013, 192).)

Even while Jerusalem was something of a backwater in late Ottoman times, it had an amateur music scene that reflected a patchwork of linguistic and faith groups. Jawharriyeh refers to a community of Jews from Aleppo (including "Haim," a violinist and an oud player), and describes the interactions between communities in festivities. He presents himself as a major contributor to this hedonistic scene, shaped by nights of reveling and singing above the accompaniment of his oud. The local scene was often enriched by visitors (Jawharriyeh refers to an Armenian oud plyer he admired, called "Sisaq") and periodically invigorated further by distinguished visitors from Egypt. As a boy, Jawharriyeh heard Sheikh Salama Hijazi, for instance, who came from Cairo in 1908 to perform with musicians and the theater director Jurji Abyad (Tamari and Nassar 2013, 72–73). Of even deeper impact perhaps were the musicians who mingled with the locals on the street and contributed to the intertwined worlds of locals and settlers. This extract from Jawharriyeh's diary deserves quotation, referring so evocatively to the Syrian musician Muhammad al-Ashiq (1885–1925), who lived for some years in

Egypt and released dozens of records:

Singer and 'ud player Muhammad al-'Ashiq used to come to Jerusalem in the summer, and make arrangements with the owners of the Hospice Cafe, which is located opposite the Austrian Hospice. He would sit on a wooden platform at one of the corners of the main road crossing opposite the Hospice, and sing with his affectionate voice and play the 'ud, while people sat around him and on every street pavement in that quarter, silent and mesmerised, drinking beverages and coffee, smoking waterpipes and cheering him, particularly during the Ramadan nights on which he sang exceptionally well until the cannon was heard. (Tamari and Nassar 2013, 35)

Under British Mandate rule, popular artists visited, including the celebrated Egyptian singer, actress, and nightclub owner Badia Masabni, who brought her band, which included oud player Shehada, a Jew from whom Jawharriyeh learned an Egyptian melody. When the British established the Palestine Broadcasting Service, the musical traffic in and out of Jerusalem increased further, but it also consolidated music into established forms that emphasized the divisions between the various communities. Airtime was divided between Arabic, English, and Hebrew language broadcasting, and

there was intense rivalry between the Arabic and Hebrew sections. In the Arabic section, the oud was a core instrument in smaller and larger studio groups, which were made up of local musicians (such as Jawharriyeh's brother Tawfiq) in combination with musicians originally from Syria and Egypt. The PBS was intended by the British as a propaganda machine, but Arab musicians managed to retain control over the music played in the Arabic Section (Beckles Willson 2013, 170–77).

The increasingly hardening divisions between groups were a particular challenge for those who fit none of the categories exclusively. Oud player Ezra Aharon (Azuri Harun), a Jewish refugee from Iraq, had been one of the first composers of music for nightclubs that sprung up in Baghdad toward the end of the Ottoman era (Kojaman 2001). He had also been part of the Iraqi delegation at the Cairo Congress of 1932, even though as an oud player he was not part of the old Baghdad tradition ostensibly represented there. In Palestine, he struggled to find a space in which to work, and avoided notating his own compositions for fear that others would use them without paying him.

After Aharon's first performance to a small Jewish circle in Jerusalem, he was advised that in order to find himself an audience he needed to incorporate the (new, modern) Hebrew language in his work (Beckles Willson 2013, 203–4). With some help he managed to do this, and Hebraist David Yellin presented him in a series of concerts in a larger venue. But this investment alienated him from local Arab musicians, who were suffering from the British rule that favored immigrant Jewish populations from Europe. Jawharriyeh regarded Aharon's insertion of Hebrew texts in Arab *muwashshah*s as "malicious" and said that musicians mocked him for it.

Over time, Aharon was able to carve out a professional niche in the Palestine Broadcasting Service and continued composing music for Hebrew texts. Ultimately he contributed to the cultivation of new "Oriental Jewish" music that could be understood as rooted in Palestine thanks to its basis in *maqam*. The musical culture brought by refugees from Europe could not claim such roots, but it dominated nonetheless. Among European Jewish settlers, there was deep hostility toward refugees from the East—Jews from Yemen as well as Iraq. Life was extremely difficult for immigrants such as Aharon.

Our valued local chronicler Jawharriyeh fled Jerusalem shortly after the 1947 partition, and himself became a refugee in Beirut. It was to be some years before he managed to replace the oud that he had left behind.

Fig. 77. Jawa Manla, Syrian oud player now living in the Netherlands.

Fig. 78. Instruments that travel, whether they like it or not...

35. OUDS IN THE MOVIES

Egypt's first talkie was released in 1932, and within a year, Mohammed Karim's film *Al-warda al-baida* ('The White Rose') was out featuring the young actor, composer, singer and oud player Abd al-Wahhab. Al-Wahhab played the part of an impoverished young man who had a series of trysts with the daughter of Ismail Pasha and attempted to elevate himself in her father's eyes by singing and playing at the opera house. This movie marked the start of a new genre for Egyptian cinema—romantic musical comedies—one which was to become enormously popular as the industry boomed in subsequent decades.

While al-Wahhab was fundamental to the earliest music films in Egypt, it was a younger immigrant musician who became most closely associated with them, namely the Syrian Farid al-Atrash. During a career in which he starred in thirty-one movies and composed some three hundred songs he became a sex symbol for the Arab world, embodying a new, modern model of romantic masculimity (Zuhur 2003). Frequently he plays a character who is a professional musician whether appearing on stage or singing on the radio. These movies portray a (quasi-biographical) tension between a musician's dedication to art and the desire for a stable human relationship and family. Oud playing is usually an accompaniment to spell-binding singing (young women sit at Farid's feet in wonder), reinforcing the historical association between the oud and seduction. In *Ayiza Atagawwiz* ("I want to get married"), meanwhile, the oud is also part of a comical scene. Farid is asleep with co-star and singer Nur al-Huda when they are discovered by another suitor of al-Huda, and he then is held at gunpoint in the wardrobe, playing oud without his pants.

Farid al-Atrash in "I want to get married"

Figs. 79 Farid al-Atrash (a) in Ayiza Atagawwiz (b) with Faten Hamamah in Lahn Al-Khouloud, (c) in concert, (d) photographer untraced.

Farid's style of playing in concert, which was virtuosic and flamboyant, was surely influenced by his career in film. Not only his carismatic physical relationship with the instrument—sometimes playing standing up—but also his extravagantly-ornate oud, were surely planned to please the crowd. His capacity for capturing audience attention, and for triggering cries of approval at the end of sections of music, seems to have been unrivalled. He developed a particular texture of scales and tremolo that he employed like a refrain towards the end of his taqasims that sent his listeners wild. He may have been the first to transplant this idiomatic guitar figuration onto the oud.

Farid al-Atrash Taqasim's taqasim 'refrain'

Fig. 80. Article about the lifestyle of Bahiga Hafez, a pioneering woman in Egyptian cinema (actress, director, composer, costume designer and editor), whose oud playing is rarely mentioned. Al-Kawakeb, Cairo, 6 June 1932, p.9.

Outside Egypt, the oud has rarely been so important in movies, but has often been a significant ingredient in soundtracks. The Nubian Hamza El Din played for *The Black Stallion* (1979), for example, a story in which a boy is shipwrecked on a desert island with only an Arab horse to keep him company. And ouds occasionally appear as exotic markers, as in the American action comedy based on Verne's novel *Around the World in 80 Days* (2004). Here Arnold Schwarzenegger plays the role of Prince Hapi and performs on a highly-ornate Arab oud in his palace in Istanbul while surrounded by twirling belly dancers.

One remarkable movie has placed the *oud* at the heart of the story, and that is Ben Sharrock's *Limbo* (2020). It focuses on a young musician from Syria who is a refugee on a remote Scottish island. Somehow he has managed to arrive there with his grandfather's oud, which he carries around in its coffin-like case throughout the movie, not feeling able to take it out and play it. The instrument symbolises all that is lost yet carried around as an inexpressible weight. Just at the end, he is finally able to recover a sense of his identity and he plays a concert.

Fig. 81a, b, c. Stills from Limbo, directed by Ben Sharrock, starring Amir El-Masry (2020).

36.   THE OUD AND THE BELLY DANCE: AMERICAN ORIENTS

Among the communities already established in America when the large waves of refugees began arriving as the Ottoman Empire collapsed were Christian Arabs from the eastern Mediterranean—the region of today's Palestine, Israel, Lebanon, and Syria. They had social gatherings called *haflat*, and also *mahrajanat*, festivals that lasted for as many as three days. The church was an organizer of these and a force in the community, and there were various other groups and charitable bodies who played a role as well. These events were social and not commercial, supporting a sense of social belonging, while supporting and developing music that was cherished by the Arabs living within and alongside American styles of entertainment and socialization (A. Rasmussen 1992, 64–65).

While these informal events continued, the commercial world of recordings must have started to make itself felt in the 1920s. But the real changes came only in the late 1940s and the 1950s in particular, when a series of nightclubs opened that catered not only to the immigrant community, but to cosmopolitan American audiences. Club Zahra (founded in Boston in 1952) and then Club Morocco, and Club Kayam (also in Boston) each had a band that was multiethnic, drawing on the broader immigrant groups of the Eastern Mediterranean—Armenian, Greek, and Turkish. The female dancers were increasingly important to these clubs; the Lebanese singer and dancer Morocco (after whom the club was named) sang Arabic, Turkish, and Greek songs and performed *raqs-sharki* (the so-called belly dance) with other women she trained. By the 1960s there were twelve such nightclubs in Greek Town in Manhattan, and restaurants gradually metamorphosed into cabarets to appeal to Americans who were cultivating fresh interests in Islamic art, rugs, and household paraphernalia brought home from travels abroad (A. Rasmussen 1992, 66ff.).

The musicians combined their various approaches to mode and rhythm, along with their instruments. Arab violinists and percussionists played with Turkish *qanun* players, Greek bouzouki players, and Armenian oud players. As recordings make clear, the sounds that captured the target audience's imagination were oboes, clarinets, and flutes—along with the fundamental *darbuka*. The service of music to dance was fundamental; the vocal, unmeasured, exploratory *taksim*s were replaced by improvisations to rhythms such as *tsifteteli*, each jerk contributing to a further slippage of the near-transparent veil of the dancer.

However, the oud was also fundamental to this movement, in part because it was central to music that the musicians themselves made, and also because it could occasionally be part of the theater. A 1958 recording for Decca featured the Armenian-Greek oud player Marko Melkon Alemsherian sitting in a plush, overtly oriental setting, surrounded by semi-clad female dancers. Yet more extreme was the cover of *The Magic Carpet*, with actor-singer-oud player Mohammad el Bakkar sitting with his oud on a carpet, with semi-clad female coffee-pourers. Melkon, at least, was an accomplished oud player whose solo recordings reveal a strong grasp of *makam* and the aesthetics of the eastern Mediterranean. But he and el Bakkar, along with many other immigrants, were maximizing their own commercial potential as "orientals," presenting themselves in exactly the stereotypes that had been created over centuries by eastward-looking Europeans and Americans and their highly disseminated literature and film. Today the oud of el Bakkar is preserved in the Metropolitan Museum of Art in New York City, bequeathed by Rosalind K. Frey, whose husband Sidney founded the label on which el Bakkar recorded, Audio Fidelity, which originally focused on Jewish music. What led the Brooklyn-based luthier Toufighe Jahromi to build an octagonal face we may never know.

Mohammad el Bakkar: "The Magic Carpet"

Fig. 82. Record sleeve of Hi-Fi Adventure in Asia Minor. Decca Records, 1958.

Next page: Fig. 83. Record sleeve of The Magic Carpet.
Audio Fidelity Inc, 1958.

37.   ARMENIANS IN AMERICA

Although the oud has a crucial part to play in the lives of many Arab-Americans, it is the Armenian communities of America that contributed most consistently to the commercial spheres of American oud playing for most of the twentieth century.

Udi Hrant Kenkulian: Saba Taksim

The half-Greek Marko Melkon mentioned in the previous chapter was surely influential. But perhaps even more important was the inspirational model of the blind Armenian survivor of the genocides in Istanbul, Udi Hrant Kenkulian (1901–1978). Hrant made a series of visits to America, starting in 1950 (Alajaji 2015, 67–71). On the first visit, he made some recordings and played in no less than five important venues with large Armenian populations—New York City, Boston, Detroit, Los Angeles, and Fresno. His performances and recordings were models for second-generation musicians such as multi-instrumentalist John Bilezikjian (1948–2015). During the 1940s and 1950s, first-generation performers could be heard at Armenian-run resorts in the Catskill Mountains in New York State. There were earlier groupings as well, some formed around (Ottoman-style) coffee houses that seem to have served the new immigrant communities struggling to make ends meet (Alajaji 2015, 144). First-generation immigrant oud player Mary Goshtigian performed in Fresno, California, and her image and *taksim* were captured by American ethnomusicologist Sidney Robertson Cowell (1903–1995) (Goshtigian 1939). Robertson identified her as a "sophisticated" player of the oud "from night clubs in Istanbul." One relatively well-documented band was the Aslanian Orchestra (its name taken from the violinist Jack Aslanian), based in Fresno but performing up and down California's San Joaquin Valley in the 1930s and 1940s, for weddings, funerals, and dances.

By the 1950s, second-generation performers were making their mark, most obviously with developments of Anatolian dances and Armenian or Turkish songs, learned in the contexts described above and adapted for the Armenian-American experience. There was a band called Nor-Ikes in New York (the oud player was Chich Gaminian) and one called Aramites in Boston, and then the New York-based Kef Time Band, formed in 1963 by Richard Hagopian (b. 1941) (Alajaji 2015, 79ff.). By then "kef" had emerged as the central genre of these various Armenian bands. It combined instruments associated with the former Ottoman world (oud, *kanun, doumbek*) with guitar, clarinet, and keyboards; it drew on Anatolian rhythms and modes, and mixed-language lyrics. But it often drew more broadly on the Ottoman world of emigrant people too; musicians were not only of Armenian descent, but also Assyrian, Greek, Lebanese, and Sephardic. While this music was recorded commercially, it was still played in community centers, churches, and homes.

Fig. 84. Mary Goshtigian. Courtesy of W.P.A. California Folk Music Project collection (AFC 1940/001), American Folklife Center, Library of Congress.

In 1964, two Armenian-American oud players represented "Armenian" music at the World's Fair in New York: John Berberian and George Mgrdichian (1935–2006). Mgrdichian is a striking case, having trained classically on clarinet at the Julliard School of Music in New York City, he turned his hand to oud, reputedly in order to spread its appeal (and perhaps to carve a professional niche for himself). His virtuosity seems to have been outstanding among his fellow Armenian-Americans, and he was likely one of the earliest to start playing European classics on oud (a famous anecdote refers to a Handel oboe concerto). Both Berberian and Mrgdichian contributed fundamentally to integrating the oud into the American world of jazz-fusion and contributing powerfully to the "oriental jazz" niche. What "oriental" meant exactly was a function of the market; even *Middle Eastern Rock* featuring Berberian on oud in 1969 was marketed with a picture of a camel painted on a female belly.

But what happened to the trauma of the genocide and forced displacement in this embrace of styles so deeply associated with Ottoman times? From the 1950s to the 1970s, at least, music seems to have provided a way in which a new sense of being Armenian—and having a home in North America—could be explored, consolidated, and celebrated. At a safe distance from Turkey, at least, the oud was central to this process, although it was a very partial reflection of Armenia itself, and increasingly distinct from musical practices in the Armenian Republic. The oud is not generally played or liked by Armenians in the Caucasus—where associations with neighboring Turkey are perhaps too strong and where the double-reed wind instrument called the *duduk* is more significant (Kassabian 2013, 30). So the Armenian oud world we are exploring here is really an Armenian-American oud world, a forced transplantation and subsequent transformation of Ottoman culture, which is now at odds with the listening habits and needs of Armenians in the homeland.

Hard on the heels of Berberian and Mgrdichian, Ara Dinkjian (b. 1958) was the next Armenian-American to make a mark. In line with the increasingly globalized music business, his career was more wide-ranging internationally than those of his predecessors. He emerged from deep inside the Armenian-American community; his earliest experiences were providing *darbuka* accompaniment to his father, a singer of Armenian song and liturgy. As a child he also accompanied Berberian and Mgrdichian, and for decades he played organ for the Armenian Apostolic Church. Compositions for his band Night Ark have drawn on the diverse strands of his musical experience to appeal to today's cosmopolitan world music audiences. But in 2013 he released an intriguingly intimate album, *Conversations with Manol* (Dinkjian 2013). This explored the sonorities of the oud alone, and indeed an oud that had deep historical significance for him as a son of the Armenian diaspora; it was made in 1907 by Emmanuel Venios (who went by the name Manol) in Ottoman Istanbul (see Chapter 24). The choice was a distinct one—reaching back into the Greek, or broader Christian community of Ottoman Istanbul—and exploring the resonances of an old instrument by a celebrated historical luthier, rather than a contemporary one.

Ara Dinkjian "Elements" from Conversations with Manol

Fig. 85. Oud made by Emmanuel Venios (Manol) in 1907, owned by and played by Ara Dinkjian on his album Conversations with Manol.

The history of Armenian luthiery has had a continuing trajectory since the genocide, albeit a more dispersed one than the history of Armenian oud playing. Some makers managed to stay in Istanbul—the celebrated Onnik Karipyian Küçüküner, for example. However, Armenian oud making flourished most obviously in Lebanon and Syria, where one of the most celebrated was Sumbat Der Bedrossian (whose son Garabed Der Bedrossian followed in his footsteps).

Leon Istanbuli was a Lebanon-based oud maker whose name belies his earlier life in Istanbul (see figure 56 for an example). Lebanon-based Dikren Najarian's craft was picked up by his grandson Viken Najarian, who finally brought the tradition to America in 1975, when he emigrated and settled in California—where he remains a sought-after luthier.

Fig. 86. Oud by Garabed Der Bedrossian, 1959.

38.   LISTENING DIFFERENTLY: THREE "REVIVALS"

Despite the 1969 album cover with the belly dancer festooned with a camel mentioned above, there were some social and creative movements developing in the 1960s that led many Europeans and Americans to realize that the oud did not need to be all about exoticism and eroticism. They can be understood collectively as forms of "revival," although they were rather distinct from one another.

The first was perhaps the attempt by Greeks to recover their Ottoman heritage. It seems to have begun with a new interest in aspects of Orthodox theology, which was not only theoretical, but involved a new fascination with monasticism and spirituality, and was combined with a form of leftist youth politics. Church music practices turned away from piano accompaniments of harmonized or polyphonic chanting and embraced monodic chant. A central figure was Simon Karas (1903–1999), who backed up his innovative teaching with extensive research (Kallimopoulou 2009, 35ff.). Reaching back to Orthodox chant traditions, and their theoretical underpinning of eight untampered modes (*echoi*) enabled him to claim an ancient and deep tradition of Greek music on which the region's "other" traditions were all based.

Most obviously that was music by then associated with the people of neighboring Turkey, but his theory essentially encompassed the entire region, and so included the Persians as well.

Karas was director of the Department of National Music in the State Radio, which was formed in 1937 under the dictatorship of Metaxas, for over three decades. During that time he was able to build a bridge between folk song and Orthodox chant, which consolidated his theoretical work in sound. His Radio Orchestra was made up of players who lived in Athens but came originally from Epirus (northern Greece, Albania), Koúlouri (the island now called Salamis), and Istanbul. The oud player was the Armenian we encountered in Chapter 32, Hagop Stambulyan/Agapios Tompoullis. His choir was trained in Byzantine chant, but also in folk songs—most likely using the aesthetics of the former to shape its singing of the latter. Karas's work contributed strongly to the notion that part of the Ottoman legacy should be recovered from the Turks because it belonged, somehow, to the Greeks.

This deeply nationalist renegotiation of Ottoman, Arab, and even Persian legacies influenced younger generations, even while they sought to express their Greekness in their own way. A key moment can be traced to the mid-1980s in the album called *Powers of the Aegean*, released by the recently formed band of the same name (Kallimopoulou 2009, 86–88). The twenty-four-year-old Hristos Tsiamoulis played oud, flanked by other young Greek musicians playing instruments of folk traditions that had largely fallen out of use in Athens—the Pontic lyre and flute, for instance. The repertoire was primarily historical, including traditional songs from Greece and Asia Minor, and *rebetiko*. Yet their goal was not so much historical as contemporary; the musicians also drew on their own background in rock and pop, and their audience was the 1980s youth culture. They sought to make traditions meaningful to themselves.

At the same time, the stylistic references were largely Greek or drawn from the melting pot of Ottoman times (Kallimopoulou 2009, 92–109). The function of the oud in songs seems in part to displace the by then typical use of the bouzouki, which doubled the melody or played in parallel thirds with it. (This essentially recovered the oud's role that the bouzouki had taken over in the 1930s.) Also, the oud playing was very distinct from the more lyrical style of oud playing that had grown up in the meantime in Turkey (such as that of Cinuçen Tanrıkorur discussed in Chapter 31). It seems based on imitation of historical styles rooted in the Ottoman era, whether the playing of Melkon, Kenkulian, or Bacanos. It pulsates in a motoric style; there is a lot of tremolo. It is repetitive in its use of melodic motives, and it is percussive.

The players nevertheless sought a very different ethos from the one they associated with the few oud-playing environments that still existed in Greece, which were for amateurs and people who wanted to dance. They associated themselves with a young, educated, urban circle. And this combined very well—in the cultural politics of the time—with the vocal styles, which included choral drones indebted to Byzantine chant.

This "new Greek" approach was developed in several directions, including in Tsiamoulis's own work toward archiving the repertoire of *Romioí*—Byzantine and Turkish Christians from the Ottoman times—and the associated interest with building an "authentically Greek" oud-playing style. This was one way of responding to the relative neglect, by Turkish musicians, of the non-Muslim Ottoman heritage. But there have been other ways to respond as well. Some musicians in Greece took a critical view of the nationalist ethos—and its associated aesthetic—and took a broader approach that sought direct exchange with musicians in Turkey and beyond. This, ultimately, has probably been more long-lasting for the oud in Greece. One of the biggest influences has been Ross Daly, a world musician who settled in Greece in the 1970s. He has worked consistently on learning and recovering traditional music but has looked well beyond the national space and has encouraged his students to do the same.

Today there are numerous Greek oud players who align their playing most strongly with the teaching of Yurdal Tokcan, thanks to his regular presence at the summer courses on Crete run under the auspices of Daly's Labyrinth Musical Workshop. This is on some level a recovery of Greek and Turkish interaction and intermingling, now across state lines. And there is other intermingling in Greece that reminds us in a different way of the Ottoman legacy. Oud player Haig Yazdjian (b. 1959) was born to refugee Armenian parents in Aleppo, but moved to Greece at twenty-one, looking for a better life (Atzakis 2013, 285). While working as a guitarist on the Arab-Athenian scene, he was asked why he didn't play Arab music, and the oud. It made him realize he knew no Arab traditional music and had no understanding of *maqam*. In time he was to become an important oud-playing figure on the Greek and international ambient and fusion scene, both as a soloist and in bands with Greek musicians. Many people hope that such figures might, through their collaborations and repertoire choices, come to illuminate new paths beyond the continuously contested Armenian-Greek-Turkish interactions.

Another significant "revival" for the oud was also a consequence of a very broad cultural shift. Europe's Early Music Movement may be understood as a response to over-rapid urbanization, technical progress (at the expense of human life), cultural homogenization, and environmental anxiety. Perhaps it had a strong element of nostalgia. However one frames it, some classical musicians returned to outdated instruments such as the harpsichord, removed metal strings from instruments and replaced them with gut, adopted a lower pitch for tuning, and developed a lighter playing style. Others sought to recover repertoires that had been neglected, including those of the so-called medieval period, which had been suppressed along with the populations who were banished at the time—Arabs and Jews in particular.

This idea was not entirely new. Already in 1929, the early music innovator Arnold Dolmetsch traveled to Morocco in order to refresh his performance practice. But there was some systematic change underway. The American Thomas Binkley (1932–1995), cofounder of the group Studio der frühen Musik in Munich, Germany, attempted to revitalize European music by incorporating not only *darbuka* and tambourines but also the bowed *rabab* into his recordings. Binkley drew his ideas from the work of Henry George Farmer among others, who had traveled in India, Turkey, and North Africa, and referred to the new style as "Arabic" or "southern." As Reynolds noticed, the musicians were not able to incorporate aspects of the appropriated traditions effectively, because they were unable to elaborate and ornament melodies (2009, 186).

Salman Shukur—oud

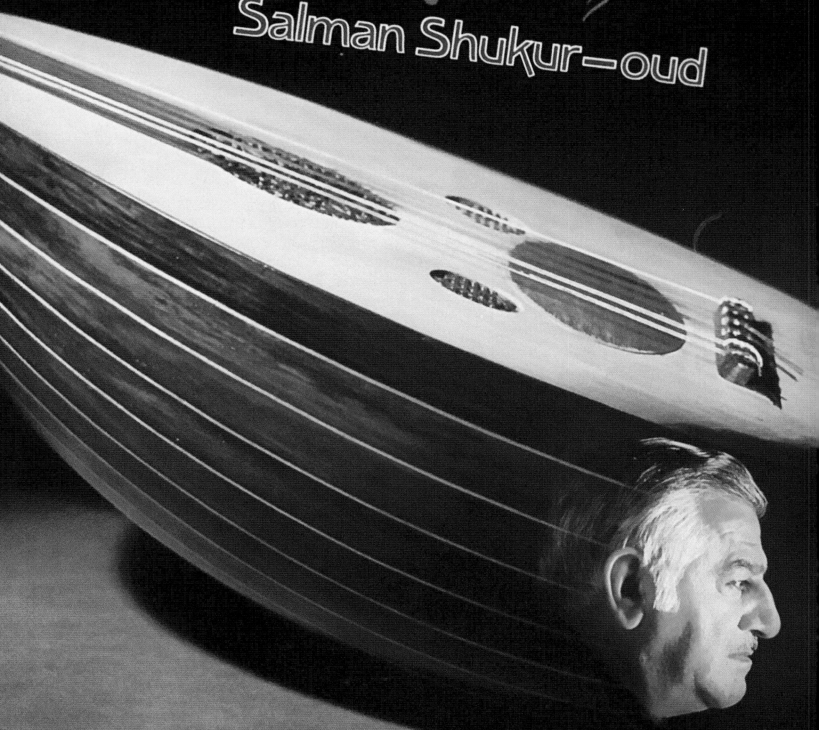

Fig. 87. The cover of Iraqi player Salman Shukur's recording Oud (Decca, 1977) won its designer, Laurie Richards, prize for best sleeve in the Classical category of the New Musical Express annual Awards to The British Music Industry in 1978.

The work of Spaniard Gregorio Paniagua was more pioneering in comparison, and in particular an innovative vinyl recording in 1969. This presented Paniagua's own ensemble, Atrium Musicae, performing twelfth- and thirteenth-century troubadour songs on one side, and Abd al-Sadiq Shiqara's ensemble from Tetouan (Morocco) performing traditional repertoire of Tetouan on the other (G. Paniagua, Atrium Musicae, and Shiqara 1969). We cannot, alas, identify the oud player in the Moroccan ensemble, because the individual names of players do not appear on the record sleeve—unlike the players of Paniagua's ensemble. But on listening, we hear his playing as fundamental to both sustaining the melody and the rhythmic drive of the ensemble. By 1977, Atrium Musicae had undertaken enough study to attempt to present North African repertoire themselves, and both Eduardo and Luis Paniagua, multi-instrumentalist members of the ensemble, played oud (G. Paniagua 1977).

However, they stopped short of including the most fundamental element of all (for North Africa, where the repertoire was so celebrated), namely the human voice. They also neglected the rhythmic qualities of the music as it was performed in North Africa. It is clear that the level to which Europeans could transform their own practice was quite limited, and there was probably an ideological framework that held them back.

As the liner notes of the 1969 recording claim, the Andalusian repertoire (played by the Moroccans) was a "clearly Spanish musical product" (Pla and de Larrea 1969, 15). In truth, even if influenced by Spanish musicians, it had been banished with the expulsion of Arabs. In a sense, and very much in line with the Greek revival, this revival was (initially at least) about creating a different (Spanish) self.

However, rather like the Greek case, some collaborations have explored entanglements more deeply. In the 1980s, Spanish musicians traveled to Tangiers to study with musicians there, and the resulting recordings (with Spaniard Luis Delgado on oud) reveal Europeans gaining a greater understanding of North African traditions. But more interesting, perhaps, were the joint ensembles, in which Spanish and North African musicians came together. In 1999, the Sudanese oud player Wafir Sheikh el-Din played with Paniagua's ensemble on the disc *Jardín de al-Andalus. Música Arabigo-Andaluza de la Sevilla Medieval* (E. Paniagua et al. 1999). There is still a big question about this "revival," given what we know of music of the twelfth century—most characteristically oud and voice or oud and *rabab* duos—and the larger ensembles that had emerged in North Africa in the nineteenth century as a result, at least in part, due to European influence. The Spanish "revival" of Andalusia tends to ignore the historical changes that have taken place in North Africa in the intervening centuries— rather as the Greek revival wanted to claim that folk music and Byzantine chant were almost the same. And yet the project has allowed for an intermingling of musicians that was surely a part of life, in those past times.

The third revival that has given the oud a new hearing has been the American folk movement. From the 1940s onward, various artists (often engaged with peace and labor movements) took to performing traditional American songs or dance music with acoustic guitar (rather than the amplified guitar that was by then prominent in jazz and rock 'n' roll contexts). One consequence of this interest was the Newport Folk Festival, an annual event based in Rhode Island that originated in 1959. It was to become a showcase not only for the burgeoning American folk music scene but also for musical diversity more broadly, and in 1964 it was the stage for the American debut of Nubian Egyptian singer and oud player Hamza El Din (1929–2006).

Hamza El Din: "Shortunga"

El Din had trained as an engineer in Cairo and also studied Arabic music at the King Fouad Institute of Middle Eastern Music. But the Newport performance was a turning point for his career and for the career of the oud in America. Within seven years of this debut, El Din had released three solo albums in the US. He went on to perform with American rock band the Grateful Dead, as well as the American string quartet Kronos Quartet, and played for several film scores and theater plays. His career reveals America taking a less conventionally orientalist interest in the oud.

There is a particularly interesting "revival with a revival" in the case of El Din. Very much in line with the original grassroots ideals of the Newport Festival, El Din had transformed his oud playing through community interactions. He had traveled with his oud to Aswan, in southern Egypt, in order to capture the music of communities of Nubians who were to be forcefully displaced in the interest of dam construction. By learning their songs, and performing them elsewhere, he both renewed his oud playing— and distinguished it from the Cairo trends that he had studied. He also used it to reflect on a power struggle brought about by modernization and industrialization.

Perhaps what is most significant about these three revivals is that they involved the oud shifting position from something that was relevant only in the past to something that was important to the present and the future. As theorist Arif Dirlik put it, there was a "willingness to listen" to traditions that had been excluded from the experiential worlds of Europe and America. They were increasingly recognized as an integral part of a transforming modernity (Beckles Willson 2019b).

Unsurprisingly, this new listening influenced the world of recording. A new interest emerged in archiving traditional music on record, and by the 1970s it represented a curating trend. Shaped by ideals from academic circles, archives, and museums, it was increasingly led by organizations such as UNESCO and the International Council for Traditional Music (ICTM). Vinyl recordings were frequently accompanied by studies of the sound, and the ethos was encyclopedic.

Over time, a need emerged to represent Arab music. The approach taken was simplistic, but effective: following the model offered by Ravi Shankar, whose recordings on sitar had been in circulation since the early 1960s and had come to "represent India." Essentially, the actors involved looked for a figure who could represent Arab music in the same way. The figure they found was Iraqi Munir Bashir, whose brother Jamil we discussed in Chapter 31. The timing was perfect for Munir, who was to become the most influential oud player of the twentieth century.

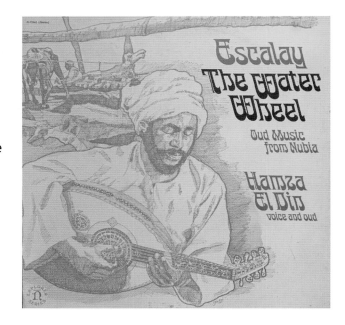

Fig 88. Record sleeve of Hamza El Din's The Water Wheel (Elektra Nonesuch, 1971)

39.   AN INVISIBLE NETWORK AND THE GROWTH OF A LEGEND

The main actors in the network were Simon Jargy, Professor of Islamic and Arab Studies at the University of Geneva, Poul Rovsing Olsen, composer, ethnomusicologist, Keeper of the Danish Folklore Archives and Chairman of the International Council for Traditional Music, and Jean-Claude Chabrier, independent researcher (Beckles Willson 2019b, 464ff.). They were to be joined in time in their promotion of Bashir by Hassan Touma, a Palestinian musicologist based in Germany, and the Syrian-French Sherif Khadnazar, Director of the Maison de la Culture in Rennes, France.

Jargy and Olsen seem to have made initial contact with Bashir in 1970 (when he was based in Beirut working for the music distribution company established by his older brother, Jamil), and they invited him to Europe for three solo concerts, which took place in 1971 in Geneva, Holstebro (Denmark), and Versailles (France). Shortly afterward, he released a vinyl recording of the Geneva concert with liner notes by Jargy, and then another vinyl recording made in Beirut in the following year, again with notes by Jargy. By 1974 Bashir was in Europe again to perform at the first Festival des Arts Traditionnels in Rennes, organized by Khadnazar. In 1977 he was back performing in Geneva. This career development was completely new, and might seem astonishing were it not for the promotional material and infrastructure that supported it. This allows us to sense the shifts taking place in Europe that made the oud so vital.

Fig. 89. Record sleeve of Munir Bashir's 1971 recital in Geneva, published in France by Pathé (disk undated).

With their varying backgrounds and interests, the group promoting Bashir understood his value in divergent ways. Jargy and Chabrier took a broadly orientalist perspective, building a rhetorical connection that spanned eleven centuries in order to link Bashir with the Abbasid court musician (and slave traders!) Ishaq al-Mawsilli and Ziryab. The main conceptual reference point for Bashir's performances was *maqam*, which was even less familiar to audiences than was the oud. Jargy drew freely on mythology, legend, and centuries-old Islamic cosmologies to claim that *maqam* originated in the twelve springs of water flowing from the rock in the Sinai desert struck by Moses. The oud, he explained, had been the physical basis for theorizing *maqam*, and was evidence of the divine status of music. His spiritual claims were part of a wider concern clear in the work of Chabrier as well: Islamic societies, they felt, did too little to sustain the Christian cultures in their midst.

Munir Bashir: Taqsim Kurd

Fig. 90. Record sleeve of Jamil Bashir's award-winning album Luth Traditionnel (Pathé, 1974).

The perspective of Olsen, by then an experienced ethnomusicologist with particular knowledge of the Gulf states, was primarily musical-encyclopedic. Rather than anchoring Bashir in the ancient past, or in religion, he presented Bashir as an innovative developer of Arab musical traditions, a musician striving to endow them with new relevance. Olsen's interest in positioning Bashir's work as a part of a developing situation, shaped by an individual in the present, was in tune with a trend in which Europe looked critically at its own colonial heritage and sought to transform itself.

The writing of leading Parisian music critic, ethnomusicologist, and composer Maurice Fleuret, who had a long-standing interest both in new European art music and musical traditions of Africa and Asia, is telling. In his appreciation of Bashir published in 1975, he identified a need for Europe to develop a new form of "hearing" to rid itself of its superiority complex and prejudices. Listening to Arab music was key, because while the music of India, Iran, and Indonesia was already accepted and supported in Europe, Arab music was still heard with prejudice (Fleuret 1975). Fleuret even made a connection between the most progressive music of the time, the so-called avant-garde, and music of the East, because they each demanded new forms of listening. Although he repeated Jargy's invocation of Moses and encircled Bashir and

his ensemble in divine *maqam*-inspiration, his main point was a post-colonial critique.

Bashir was quick to learn how to cater to his new audiences in Europe. He switched, for instance, from wearing a modern suit and tie to appearing in a traditional full-length robe, the *gandoura*. This enabled him to represent a loosely defined spiritual figure, to enact the role and the perspective according to which, as he put it in interview, "the Orientals in general, and Arabs in particular, are spiritually inclined people," and to note that the Orient was where "the great religious systems originated" (M. Bashir 1975, 16–17). He also cultivated an atmosphere akin to a ritual for his concerts; prior to each piece he sat before the audience at length in silence and avoided any form of amplification.[11] He requested very low lighting and even perfume in the air—his preference was for incense, central to the Orthodox rite. Within his improvisations he left long silences and long moments of resounding strings, both of which were entirely novel in Arab concert music in general, and oud-playing traditions in particular. He also took a particularly ascetic approach to listening in the concert hall. At his first appearance in Rennes in 1974, he stopped playing to command, in Arabic, that listeners refrain from tapping in time to the music, and he threatened to stop playing if it happened again (Khaznadar 1998, 1). With this act, he diverged fundamentally from the practice of participatory listening characteristic of many traditional Arab settings and opted instead for the European concert aesthetic. Thus, even while his promoters sought to challenge Eurocentrism through him, Bashir affirmed European modernist listening regimes.

Bashir also took up the European discourses of revivals, presenting himself as the first person to resuscitate the model of instrumental soloist, lost since Ziryab and al-Farabi in the ninth century. Yet more ambitiously (or pretentiously!), in 1989 he sought to recover ancient Babylon by studying clay tablets. "Babylon was the center of the world's civilization, arts and culture," he said in an interview, "and it is right that it regain that fame again" (n.a. 1989). Bashir was proposing a revitalization of the civilized world. Its very foundations needed to be heard—and the oud was the instrument to make that possible.

These rather extravagant ideas emerged from a musician who by then had managed to achieve substantial diplomatic power in Iraq. There was little interest in traditional Arab music in Iraq in the 1970s, but when in 1973 the governing Ba'ath Party formed a new cultural council as part of a broad political consolidation, Bashir was invited back from Beirut to Baghdad to become a member. It is likely that the European construction of Bashir as the new al-Mawsili or Ziryab had

reached the homeland and fed into the new cultural politics emerging there. Certainly Iraqi strong man Saddam Hussein used this formula, historicizing himself as a leader who followed directly from Abbasid rulers (Tripp 2000, 217). Bashir was placed in charge of a new department of music in 1977 (the year his brother, Jamil, passed away) within the Iraqi National Music Committee, effectively taking charge of all the state institutions involved with music, including education, research, and performance (Hassan 2011, 201) The Iraqi National Music Committee was incorporated as a member into UNESCO's International Music Council, which connected Bashir to a global institution for the development of traditional music.

The institutional support that Bashir won led him to have a cultural-political role on a global stage; as a New York critic observed, he was like a modern-day Paderewski, the Polish pianist who became prime minister. The legends of al-Mawsili and Ziryab were no longer needed for self-orientalization, but they were useful for masking the rich historical and contemporary cultural contexts on which his creative work depended. He appeared to have been the only oud player of significance in Iraq for some ten centuries.

Iraq had several rich musical strands already, including the intensely expressive world of the vocal repertoire known as Iraqi Maqam, which was sustained by Jewish players in the traditional ensemble *chalghi* until the expulsion of the Jews (Kojaman 2001). Whereas in 1947 the Jewish community was an estimated 117,000 people, by 1952 it had almost completely disappeared, and Iraq had lost part of its richest and most highly educated population. While the musical life in particular was greatly reduced, developments in oud playing—the cultivation of the oud led by Sherif Muhiddin Targan and then Jamil Bashir—allowed it to be sustained in quite radically transformed ways. The oud was incorporated into the *chalghi*, for example. Iraqi Maqam melodies were gradually absorbed into the new sphere of solo oud performance and developed in the style of *taqsim* (improvisation). The melodic explorations of Bashir are exemplary.

It was not only this rich history that fed into Bashir's playing. There was also his oud, which, notwithstanding the historical orientalizing that surrounded his appearance, he had developed in collaboration with luthier Muhammad Fadel in the context of intense modernization. In its technical innovation, breaking away from established Arab models, this instrument comes in line with revolutionary developments in the fine arts and literature described in Chapter 25. By securing strings to the body of the instrument and raising them with a moveable "floating" bridge resting on the face, he eliminated the torsion on the face. This and other changes result in a transformed oud: the strings transfer string vibrations to the sound board in a different manner, the new bracing creates a different resonance inside the sound box, and the instrument is far louder than most ouds of the period. Paradoxically, this oud facilitated a style of playing slowly and quietly, leaving time left for atmospheric echoes and silences in the newly adapted melodies of Iraqi Maqam. Loudness may be associated with modern power in a brute sense, but this oud's powerful resonance enabled Bashir to play softly and to command attention in an apparently spiritual way. As we have seen, it had an intense appeal to European listeners.

40. DIASPORAS

The novel aspect of Bashir's and Hamza El Din's audiences was that they came from outside the cultural sphere where these musicians, and their instrument, had been at home. Since that change, numerous oud players have made an impact away from home. It is not possible to do justice to the rich tapestry of subsequent oud-playing innovations that have resulted, but four oud players have taken the instrument to distinct new audiences and deserve special mention.

One of the most influential oud players-cum-educators has been Simon Shaheen (b. 1955), who moved from Haifa to New York to study (western classical) violin in 1980. His training in both western classical music and Arab music was rare, and it shaped how he positioned himself and his oud (Tannous, n.d.). Rather than being content with the nightclub scene, he sought to raise awareness of the historical sophistication of Arab music, presenting it in concerts to non-Arab Americans. At its peak, the Near East Music Ensemble he founded in 1982 (a slightly extended *takht*) was performing around forty concerts a year, for audiences of both Arab-Americans and non-Arab listeners. His thrust was always educational, introducing the *maqam* of the repertoire to be played and providing context for the selected pieces. In collaboration with the community of Arab-Americans with whom he was performing and teaching, he worked to encourage Arab-Americans to make music themselves rather than depend on exports from back home.

Shaheen's arrival benefited from the wave of revivals discussed in Chapter 37. During the same revivals period, a number of oud players, and multi-instrumentalists who played oud, moved to Europe and the US in order to study. One was Munir Bashir, who enrolled as a composition student at the Liszt Academy in Budapest, Hungary, in 1962, but more significant for Shaheen was Ali Jihad Racy, the Lebanese musician who became a graduate student in the US in 1968. The arrival of students from the Arab world contributed to an incremental transformation of university curricula, first in parts of North America and then, tentatively, in parts of Europe. With "ethnomusicology" established as a field of study, and with the establishment of university performance groups specific to particular non-European traditions, a new market opened up for oud players seeking not only to study but also to teach or perform. In a number of cases, this has led to a greater integration of the oud in American institutions. Jihad Racy gained a professorial position at the University of California, Los Angeles, and at least two of his oud-playing American students went on to become professors at other universities, establishing Middle East ensembles and encouraging students to learn the oud.

In 1997 Shaheen and Racy collaborated to establish the Arabic Music Retreat, a private educational venture that has also contributed to the dissemination of the oud in North America. Students attend classes in *maqam* theory, ear training, and Arab music history. They also take individual instrumental lessons, participating in a *takht* and a full orchestra.

The core historical repertoire stems from Egypt, with contemporary works by the musicians teaching. This retreat, in combination with university ensembles, creates a meeting point between informal (Arab) communities of Arab music making and more structured educational programs for young people.

Fig. 91. Four players who have been particularly successful in finding new audiences for the oud. (a) Simon Shaheen (b) Anouar Brahem (photo credit Marco Borggreve) (c) Kamilya Jubran (d) Marcel Khalife.

A very different example is Lebanese oud player and composer Marcel Khalife, who has been more prolific as a composer and recording artist than Shaheen. He also attracts larger concert audiences in the Arab World and Europe, where he has toured extensively with his extended ensemble, Al Mayadine. Khalife's audiences are mainly drawn from the Arab diaspora, and they attend less for his oud playing than for his original songs, his singing, and his stance on the Palestinian cause (perhaps also his affiliation to the Communist Party). Listeners often sing along to certain songs, and it is normal for audiences to be moved to tears (which is relatively unusual in European concert halls). In his arms the oud seems to be a vehicle that both contributes to this atmosphere and facilitates his singing. His songs explore subjects close to the hearts of many Arab listeners distant from home (and whose homes are truly lost) and engage numerous listeners from beyond the Arab world who are committed to human freedom, and particularly the freedom of Palestinians.

Each of these oud players has explored new directions for the oud. Khalife took the step of writing for two ouds in combination, releasing an album recorded with oud player Charbel Rohana in 1995 called *Jadal*. Rather than playing the same melody in diversely ornamented ways, each oud player has a separate part. The duo combination may have inspired a later oud ensemble, the Trio Joubran, combining three Palestinian oud-playing brothers from the Galilee. Khalife has not hesitated to draw on western classical harmony to expand the impact of his music; his later album *Taqasim*, for instance, presents the oud as a soloist with the harmonic backing of a substantial ensemble.

Marcel Khalife and Charbel Rohana: "Jadal"

Previous Page: Figs. 92a and b. Negar Bouban and Yasamin Shahhosseini, both from Iran.

Shaheen's focus has been grounded more firmly in a sense of traditions and the possibility of developing listener appreciation of these. His albums *Turath* (Heritage) and *The Music of Mohamed Abdel Wahab* present historical repertoire, for instance. His duo album with Racy, *Taqasim: Art of Improvisation in Arabic Music,* is an intriguing development of the *taqsim* practice: here it is not a solitary meditation but a shared exploration, as the two musicians pass their melodic lines back and forth on oud and *bouzouk,* shifting through the various modal regions of three *maqam*s. Shaheen also shifted with the development of world music trends, leading an ensemble (Qantara) that could incorporate elements of jazz and flamenco, particularly when mixed with varied percussion, and guest artists playing saxophone and trumpet. Among a number of original pieces, the ensemble's 2001 album, *Blue Flame,* includes a cover of "Tea in the Sahara," a song by Sting.

Qantara: "Blue Flame"

The oud player who has had the greatest impact on the jazz-fusion scene is probably Anouar Brahem (b. 1957). At home in Tunisia, one of his innovations was carving out a space for instrumental music (distinct from the vocal *maluf* discussed in Chapter 30, and the predominance of vocal music in general)—as heard on his first album, for a trio of violin, oud, and percussion. Having created this space, and drawing on his network and education in France, he progressively expanded it, developing collaborations with a series of high-flying artists who had their own loyal listeners. Brahem was by no means the first oud player to place the oud in jazz settings—his contemporary, the Lebanese Rabih Abou-Khalil, started releasing albums earlier on and had very significant recognition. But Brahem's oud playing, especially intertwined with the playing of Norwegian saxophonist Jan Garbarek and Pakistani tabla player Ustad Shaukat Hussein on the album *Madar,* set a new level in hybrid styles that had huge appeal across the world music, jazz, and even classical worlds.

In Brahem's hands the oud was no longer an accompaniment to a voice, nor was it a soloist in a western classical sense, but an equal player in a jazz ensemble in which players alternately accompanied, riffed, and soloed rhythmic melodies. Key to his success was the elite recording space—Manfred Eicher's ECM—which worked wonders for the digital reproduction of oud resonance, not to mention the prestige of the oud in Europe.

Anouar Brahem „Bom Dia Rio"

The paths forged by Shaheen, Khalife, and Brahem can be traced as growth areas today. For engagement with historical repertoire, Mustafa Said is a reference point, his work drawing on the digitalization of nineteenth-century recordings of Arab repertoire (see also his development of oud ensembles in Chapter 7). Another is Nizar Rohana, who takes examples of taqsim (the by-now canonical recordings of al-Qasabji and al-Sunbati) as models and starting points for historically grounded composition (Rohana 2021). Tunisian Dhafer Youssef has taken the oud into the ambient sphere, while an interesting combination of pop fusion and electronic manipulation is offered by Mehdi Haddab, a Tunisian musician who has combined oud with vocoder.

Nizar Rohana: Mufradat Nahawand.

Fig. 93. Nizar Rohana.

While these three players tapped into various types of mainstream audiences, Kamilya Jubran (b. 1962) developed an audience in Europe's experimental music scene. Jubran's emergence in Europe was part of her second career—the first being as a singer and *qanun* player in the Ramallah-based band Sabreen. Since arriving in Europe in 2003 she has collaborated consistently with Werner Hasler, Swiss composer and performer of trumpet and live electronics, enabling the oud to mingle with and contribute to entirely unique sonic worlds of melody, rhythm, sound, and language. As in the case of Khalife, Jubran's voice and message are paramount, but her message is yet more critical and much more questioning. In her "Suite Nomade" (included on the album *Nhaoul* in 2012), a work composed collaboratively with bass player Sarah Murcia, she includes an erotic poem by a Bedouin, celebrating his liberty of expression (and his freedom to roam on the land of Palestine before anyone claimed it as a nation). Her gesture is amplified by her own iconoclastic style of playing and singing it. The contemporary music world is, she has said, the one in which she felt free.

Kamilya Jubran: "Laïtani"

Jubran's appearance as a female oud player has been inspiring for numerous female musicians. In her childhood home she herself had no restraints, but in Asia it remains rare for women to move publicly, as instrumentalists, beyond the accepted role of vocalist. The two iconic female singers of the twentieth century—Umm Kulthum and Fairouz—played instruments when they were young, but as mature professionals they were never seen playing. The celebrated Lebanese singer and actress Najah Salam (b. 1931) learned oud in secret, because her father (a distinguished composer and oud player himself) was against it. Jubran herself became an oud player away from her original homeland, but—as we have already seen in the cases of Iran and Tunisia—the barriers are being chipped away in some of the traditional oud-playing areas. The Egyptian Sherine Tohamy has released several albums and is a professor at Bait Al Oud in Abu Dhabi, for instance, and the Syrian Rihab Azar continues the career she was building in Damascus until the civil war, to the extent it is possible in the United Kingdom.

Fig. 94. Umm Kulthoum playing oud at the Bosphorous Casino in 1927. Copyright untraced.

AFTERWORD

In this book the oud has taken us on a journey from early Greco-Buddhist cultures of central Asia to the experimental music scene in Europe, passing through the slave world of the Arab caliphates, the rise of European imperialism, and the diasporic spread of the post-Ottoman world. We have learned how the oud has absorbed ideas about geometry and cosmology, imperial prestige and diasporic identity, and we have discovered its role in storytelling, seduction, and orientalism. There are few instruments through which such a richness of stories could be told, even though what is presented here is of course only a selection.

The most interesting questions left are about the future. What will the oud mean to people by the middle of the twenty-first century? Who will play it? Who will listen?

Answers may depend most on the multiple people learning the oud now. The oud has become an almost global instrument because it is available so widely and because so many different people feel they want to play it. To be sure, numerous Arab men turn to the oud as an expression of their identity in Europe and North America, perpetuating an established tradition. But within the dispersed Arab world there is a diversification in process. One of my oud-playing correspondents introduced herself to me as an "Arab queer woman" living in the UK. Dalia Sabry (b. 1985), a blind Jordanian, not only took it upon herself to learn the oud and took comfort in it in the face of intense social prejudice, she also became a university-level oud teacher and promotes music education for the blind. Also, the oud has spread beyond the Arab world in Asia and Africa, so the children of emigres are diverse: I have taught two Somalis, both born and raised in the UK, both interested in Somali repertoire.

Other students reach the oud through different channels. One of my pupils in London is a Kurdish woman who grew up in Sweden: she has come to love Arabic music from listening to music with her Egyptian husband. Another of my students, an American who grew up in Alaska, approached me to learn Turkish oud after having lived in Istanbul for some time. I know two Japanese women in the UK who are studying oud, one otherwise working as an architect in London and the other as a language teacher in Manchester. One English woman who contacted me recently said that music was an expression of mysticism for her, and that listening to the oud specifically brought her in touch with her spirituality: she too wanted to buy an instrument and start oud lessons.

All these students have their reasons for turning to the oud, and it would be a mistake to generalize about where the instrument is headed now. But in the difficult times in which we live today, it is surely heartening that such a range of people makes the effort to capture the potential beauty of oud playing. On some level they are all challenging themselves to bring something new to life—if not the world as we wish it could be, then at least a creativity and joy that makes every day a little better for themselves and those nearby.

LIST OF ILLUSTRATIONS

Fig. 47. Egyptian oud, pre-1839. Photo credit David San Millán. Courtesy of the Musical Instruments Museum, Brussels.

Fig. 48. Oud by Yusif al-Nahhat, 1874. Courtesy of the Royal Northern College of Music, Manchester.

Fig. 49a. Part of internal decorations of Oud by Yusif al-Nahhat, 1874. Courtesy of the Royal Northern College of Music, Manchester.

Fig. 49b. Part of internal decorations of Oud by Yusif al-Nahhat, 1874. Courtesy of the Royal Northern College of Music, Manchester.

Fig. 50. Oud arbi donated to the South Kensington Museum by Ismail Pasha, the khedive of Egypt. Photo credit by David San Millán. Copyright Horniman Museum and Gardens (object number M24.8.56/95).

Fig. 51. Rosette of Oud arbi donated to the South Kensington Museum by Ismail Pasha, the khedive of Egypt. Photo credit by David San Millán. Copyright Horniman Museum and Gardens (object number M24.8.56/95).

Fig. 52. Oud arbi donated to the South Kensington Museum by Ismail Pasha, the khedive of Egypt. Photo credit by David San Millán. Copyright Horniman Museum and Gardens (object number M24.8.56/95).

Fig. 53. Oud by Iskender Qudmany. Photo by the author.

Figs. 54a, 54b and 54c. Vintage pictures. No copyright traced.

Fig. 55. Oud made in 1908 by Emmanuel Venios (Manol), owned by Ara Dinkjian.

Fig. 56. Two ouds by Armenian makers. Instrument on the left by Leon Istanbuli (workshop in Beirut, date not visible); instrument on the right by Ali Galip (1920), whose workshop was in Istanbul.

Fig. 57a. Oud by "Mustafa," Adana 1907. Courtesy of the Swedish Museum of Performing Arts in Stockholm (object inventory number X5058).

Fig. 57b. Label from inside oud by "Mustafa," Adana 1907. Photo by the author. Swedish Museum of Performing Arts in Stockholm (Sweden), object inventory number X5058.

Fig. 58. Mass-produced ouds and bağlamas.

Fig. 59. Two modern Turkish ouds from Istanbul by Faruk Türünz and Ramazan Calay. Photo by the author.

Fig. 60. Floating-bridge oud by Muhammad Fadel, 1957. Photo by the author. Courtesy of Saad Bashir.

Fig. 61a. Oud by Rafia Arazi (1919). From the collection of Ahmad AlSalhi. Photo by Fatemah al-Fadel.

Fig. 61b. Oud by Numan Rahibe 1912. From the collection of Ahmad AlSalhi. Photo by Fatemah al-Fadel.

Fig. 62. This postage stamp from the UEA suggests a strong adherence to traditional oud playing.

Fig. 63. Oud by Ahmad Abduljalil, Kuwait, 2012. From the collection of Ahmad AlSalhi. Photo by Fatemah al-Fadel.

Fig. 64. One of the earliest writers on taksim, Dimitrie Cantemir (Kantemiroglu), commemorated on a postage stamp in Moldova, where he served as military commander in 1693 and 1710–1711.

Fig. 65. An oud owned by Muhammad al-Qasabji (unknown maker). Private collection.

Fig. 66. Yorgo Bacanos with his brother Aleko. Photo by Mustafa Karatas.

Fig. 67. Rachel Beckles Willson.

Fig. 68. Sherif Muhiddin Targan.

Fig. 69. Sherif Muhiddin Targan: vinyl record made in New York, 1925.

Fig. 70. "Samai Nahawand" by Jamil Bashir. Reproduced from Achabaka, 13 Jan 1975

Fig. 71. Yurdal Tokcan.

Fig. 72. Cinucen Tanrıkorur.

Fig. 73. Lambros Leondaritis, Rosa Eshkenazi, Dimitris Tomboulis. Uncredited photo from vinyl recording Fünf Griechen in der Hölle (Tikont 1982).

Figs. 74a and 74b. Postcard sent from Constaninople in 1929. No copyright traced.

Fig. 75. Ahmad Al Khatib, an internationally distinguished oud player born in a Palestinian refugee camp in Jordan, now living in Sweden.

Fig. 76. Wasif Jawharriyeh.

Fig. 77. Jawa Manla, Syrian oud player now living in the Netherlands.

Fig. 78. Instruments that travel, whether they like it or not...

Figs. 79. Farid al-Atrash (a) in Ayiza Atagawwiz (b) with Faten Hamamah in Lahn Al-Khouloud, (c) in concert, (d) photographer untraced.

Fig. 80. Article about the lifestyle of Bahiga Hafez, a pioneering woman in Egyptian cinema (actress, director, composer, costume designer and editor), whose oud playing is rarely mentioned. Al-Kawakeb, Cairo, 6 June 1932, p.9.

Fig. 81a, b, c. Stills from Limbo, directed by Ben Sharrock, starring Amir El-Masry (2020).

Fig. 82. Record sleeve of Hi-Fi Adventure in Asia Minor. Decca Records, 1958.

Fig. 83. Record sleeve of The Magic Carpet. Audio Fidelity Inc, 1958.

Fig. 84. Mary Goshtigian. Courtesy of W.P.A. California Folk Music Project collection (AFC 1940/001), American Folklife Center, Library of Congress.

Fig. 85. Oud made by Emmanuel Venios (Manol) in 1907, owned by and played by Ara Dinkjian on his album Conversations with Manol.

Fig. 86. Oud by Garabed Der Bedrossian, 1959.

Fig. 87. The cover of Iraqi player Salman Shukur's recording Oud (Decca, 1977) won its designer, Laurie Richards, prize for best sleeve in the Classical category of the New Musical Express annual Awards to The British Music Industry in 1978.

Fig 88. Record sleeve of Hamza El Din's The Water Wheel (Elektra Nonesuch, 1971)

Fig. 89. Record sleeve of Munir Bashir's 1971 recital in Geneva, published in France by Pathé (disk undated).

Fig. 90. Record sleeve of Jamil Bashir's award-winning album Luth Traditionnel (Pathé, 1974).

Fig. 91. Four players who have been particularly successful in finding new audiences for the oud. (a) Simon Shaheen (b) Anouar Brahem (photo credit Marco Borggreve) (c) Kamilya Jubran (d) Marcel Khalife.

Figs. 92a and b. Negar Bouban and Yasamin Shahhosseini, both from Iran.

Fig. 93. Nizar Rohana.

Fig. 94. Umm Kulthoum playing oud at the Bosphorous Casino in 1927. Copyright untraced.

Fig. 95. Three modern ouds in "Turkish" (Faruk Türünz), "Iraqi" (Dimitris Rapakousios), and "Arab" (Nazih Ghadban) styles. Photo by the author.

REFERENCES

Abdallah, Tarek. 2010. "L'évolution de l'art du 'ūd Égyptien En Solo à l'aune Du 78 Tours." La Revue Des Traditions Musicales Des Mondes Arabe et Méditerranéen 4: 53–66.

———. 2016. "Egyptian Ouds from 1800 to the 1930s." 2016. https:// oudmigrations.com/2016/11/14/ how-large-were-egyptian-ouds/.

———. 2017. "L'art du 'ūd Égyptien, de l'organologie à La Performance La Virtuosité Traditionnelle et Son Évolution à l'aune du 78 Tours." Lyon: Université Lumière Lyon2.

Abdullaev, Kazim. 2015. Buddhist Iconography of Northern Bactria. Translated by Alison Betts. New Delhi, India: Manohar Publishers & Distributors.

Alajaji, Sylvia. 2015. Music and the Armenian Diaspora: Searching for Home in Exile. Public Cultures of the Middle East and North Africa. Bloomington, Indianapolis: Indiana University Press.

Al-Ḥulaʾī, Muhammad Kāmil. 1904. Kitāb Al-Mūsīqī a-š-Šarqī [Livre Du Musicien Oriental]. Cairo, Egypt: Maktabat a-d-Dār al-ʾArabiyya li-l-kitāb.

Al-Salhi, Ahmad. 2016. "India to Kuwait." Oudmigrations.

2016. https://oudmigrations. com/2016/05/22/india-to-kuwait/.

Al-Salhi, Ahmad Ali. 2016. "Ṣaut in Bahrain and Kuwait: History and Creativity in Concept and Practice." PhD thesis, London, UK: Royal Holloway, University of London.

Arınç, Cihat, Christian Moser, and Martin Stokes. 2017. "Nostalgia and the Female Oud Player." Oudmigrations. 2017. https:// oudmigrations.com/2017/02/06/ nostalgia-for-the-female-oud-player/.

Arslan, Fazli. 2007. "Safī Al-Dīn al-Urmavī and the Theory of Music: Al-Risāle al-Sharafiyya Fī al-Nisab al-Taʾlīfiyya–Contents, Analysis, and Influences." Edited by Mohamed El-Gomati, Mohammed Abattouy, and Salim Ayduz. Foundation for Science, Technology and Civilization Limited.

Asīl Ensemble, and Mustafa Said. 2010. Asil: New Composition From the Core of Tradition. CD. Forward Music.

Atzakis, Thimios. 2013. "People of the Wood. The Ud-Istic Art from the Outskirts of Eastern Music World to Contemporary Greek Urban Culture." Ph.D. thesis, University of the Aegean.

Ayangil, Ruhi. 2008. "Western Notation in Turkish Music." Journal of the Royal Asiatic Society 18 (4): 401–47.

Barutcu, Tuba. 2019. "Taş Plak Geleneğinde Türk Müziği Kadin Ses Sanatçilarinin Müzikal Kimlik ve Müzikal Gelişimleri." Afyon Kocatepe Universitesi Akademik Muzik Arastirmalari Dergisi 5 (10): 83–107.

Bashir, Jamil. 1961. Al-ʾud Wa Tariqat Radisihi. Baghdad: Institute of Fine Arts.

Bashir, Mounir. 1978. "Musical Planning in a Developing Country: Iraq and the Preservation of Musical Identity." The World of Music 20 (1): 74–78.

Bashir, Munir. 1975. "Interview with the Iraqi Ud Virtuoso Munir Bashir." The World of Music 17 (2): 14–18.

Bates, Eliot. 2012. "The Social Life of Musical Instruments." Ethnomusicology 56 (3): 363–95.

Beckles Willson, Rachel. 2013. Orientalism and Musical Mission: Palestine and the West. Cambridge University Press.

———. 2014. "Foreword: Hearing Palestine." In The Storyteller of Jerusalem, IX–XVI. Northampton, MA: Olive Branch Press.

———. 2017. "The Oud in England." Oudmigrations. 2017. https:// oudmigrations.com/2017/01/09/the-oud-in-england/.

———. 2016f. "Adana to Stockholm." Oudmigrations. 2016f. https://oudmigrations.com/2016/03/10/adana-to-stockholm/.

———. 2016b. "Alexandria to Brussels, 1839." Oudmigrations. 2016b. https://oudmigrations.com/2016/03/02/alexandria-to-brussels-1839/.

———. 2016a. "Cairo to London." Oudmigrations. 2016a. https://oudmigrations.com/2016/03/06/cairo-to-london-1867/.

———. 2019b. "Hearing Global Modernity: The Case of the Travelling Oud." International Journal for History, Culture and Modernity 7 (1): 458–85.

———. 2019a. "Orientation through Instruments: The ʿūd, the Palestinian Home, and Kamīlyā Jubrān." The World of Music 8 (1): 23–48.

Beckles Willson, Rachel, and Negar Bouban. 2018. "The Oud in Iran." 2018. https://oudmigrations.com/2018/11/05/the-oud-in-iran/.

Beckles Willson, Rachel, and Karim Othman Hassan. 2016c. "Salman Shukur's Oud." Oudmigrations. 2016c. https://oudmigrations.com/2016/12/12/salman-shukurs-oud/.

Beckles Willson, Rachel, and Karim Othman Hassan. 2017. "Oud of a Virtuoso." Oudmigrations. 2017. https://oudmigrations.com/2017/03/13/oud-of-a-virtuoso/.

Bernard, Paul, and Franz Grenet, eds. 1991. Histoire et Cultes de l'Asie Centrale Préislamique: Sources Écrites et Documents Archéologiques. Paris, France: Centre National De La Recherche Scientifique.

Besseler, Heinrich, and Max Schneider. 1969. Musikgeschichte in Bildern. Band III: Music Des Mittelalters Und Der Renaissance. Vol. 2. Leipzig, Germany: VEB Deutscher Verlag für Musik.

Beyhom, Amine. 2020. "Dosser: Was the Early Arabian 'ud 'Fretted'?" Near Eastern Musicology Online 5 (9): 113–96.

Boudjikanian-Keuroghlian, Aïda, Roubina Artinian, and Haykazean Golēch, eds. 2009. Armenians of Lebanon: From Past Princesses and Refugees to Present-Day Community. Beirut: Haigazian University.

Boulos, Issa, Virginia Danielson, and Anne K Rasmussen, eds. 2021. Music in Arabia: Perspectives on Heritage, Mobility, and Nation. Bloomington, Indiana: Indiana University Press.

Bowers, Jane. 1986. "The Emergence of Women Composers in Italy, 1566–1700." In Women Making Music: The Western Art Tradition, 1150–1950, edited by Jane Bowers and Judith Tick, 116–67. Urbana and Chicago, USA: Springer.

Brenk, Beat, and Giovanni Chiaramonte, eds. 2010. La Cappella Palatina a Palermo. Mirabilia Italiae 17. Modena: F. C. Panini.

Brinkhurst, Emma. 2012. "Music, Memory and Belonging: Oral Tradition and Archival Engagement among the Somali Community of London's King's Cross." Ph.D. thesis, London, UK: Goldsmiths, University of London.

Brown, Howard Mayer. 1986. "Women Singers and Women's Songs in Fifteenth-Century Italy." In Women Making Music: The Western Art Tradition, 1150–1950, edited by Jane Bowers and Judith Tick, 62–89. Urbana and Chicago, USA: Springer.

Brown, Patricia Fortini. 2004. Private Lives in Renaissance Venice: Art, Architecture, and the Family. 1st ed. New Haven; London: Yale University Press.

———. 2012. "Music in Venetian Art: Seduction and Spirituality." British Academy Review 20: 21–26.

Caldwell, Maria V. 1986. "Jougleresses and Trobairitz: Secular Musicians in Medieval France." In Women Making Music: The Western Art Tradition, 1150–1950, edited by Jane Bowers and Judith Tick, 39–61. Urbana and Chicago: Springer.

Campbell, Kay Hardy. 2021. "Songstresses of Saudi Arabia." In Music in Arabia: Perspectives on Heritage, Mobility and Nation, 178–97. Bloomington, Indiana: Indiana University Press.

Castelo-Branco, Salwa El-Shawan. 2002. "Performance of the Arab Music in 20th Century Egypt: Reconciling Authenticity and Contemporaneity." In The Garland Encyclopedia of World Music: Middle East, edited by Virginia Danielson, Scott Marcus, and Reynolds Dwight, 6:299–307. New York, USA: Routledge.

Caswell, Fuad Matthew. 2011. The Slave Girls of Baghdad: The Qiyān in the Early Abbasid Era. Library of Middle East History 28. London: I. B. Tauris.

Cevher, M. Hakan. 1993. "Birinci Bölüm." In Şerif Muhiddin Targan: Hayatı, Besteciliği, Eserleri, 1–21. Turkey: Ege Üniversitesi Basımevi.

Çevik, Senem B. 2018. "Can Turkish-Armenian Music Diplomacy Emulate the Turkish-Greek Example?: Prospects and Limitations." Caucasus Survey 6 (2): 130–46.

Chabrier, Jean-Claude. 1978. "New Developments in Arabian Instrumental Music." The World of Music 20 (1): 94–109.

———. 1979. "Le Congrès International de la Musique et le Festival du 'Ud (Bagdad, 1er-7 Décembre 1978)." Revue de Musicologie 65 (1): 76.

———. 1996. "Şerif Muhiddin Haydar Hâşimî Targan, Luthiste et Compositeur. Une Confluence Culturelle Ottomane et Un Rayonnement Artistique Mondial." In Histoire Êconomique et Sociale de l'Empire Ottoman et de La Turquie (1326-1960), Actes 6'eme Congrês International, Aix En Provence,1992, edited by Daniel Panzac, 767–74. Paris, France: Peeters.

Coelho, Victor. 1992. Music and Science in the Age of Galileo. Vol. 51. Dordrecht: Springer Science & Business Media.

Congrès de musique arabe du Caire [18 CDs]. 2015. Paris: Bibliothèque nationale de France.

Coomaraswamy, Ananda K. 1928. "Notes Sur La Sculpture Bouddhique." Revue Des Arts Asiatiques 5 (4): 244–52.

Cordereix, Pascal, and Jean Lambert, eds. 2015. Congrès de musique arabe du Caire [Booklet accompanying CD box set]. Paris: Bibliothèque nationale de France.

Coryat, Thomas. 1905. Coryat's Crudities: Hastily Gobled up in Five Moneths Travells in France, Savoy, Italy, Rhetia Commonly Called the Grisons Country, Helvetia Alias Switzerland, Some Parts of High Germany and the Netherlands: Newly Digested in the Hungry Aire of Odcombe in the County of Somerset, and Now Dispersed to the Nourishment of the Travelling Members of This Kingdome. Vol. 1. Glasgow: J. MacLehose and Sons.

Cowell, Sidney Robertson. 1939. "Mary Goshtigian Playing the Oud, Seated, Portrait, Photograph. California, Fresno." California Gold: Northern California Folk Music from the Thirties Collected by Sidney Robertson Cowell. 1939. https://www.loc.gov/item/2017701341/.

Craig-McFeely, Julia. 2002. "The Signifying Serpent: Seduction by Cultural Stereotype in Seventeenth-Century England." In Music, Sensation, and Sensuality, edited by Linda P. Austern. Routledge.

Danielson, Virginia. 2021. "The Oil Economy and the Perpetuation of Musical Heritage in Abu Dhabi." In Music in Arabia: Perspectives on Heritage, Mobility and Nation, 34–51. Bloomington, Indiana: Indiana University Press.

Danielson, Virginia, Scott

Marcus, and Reynolds Dwight, eds. 2002. The Garland Encyclopedia of World Music: Middle East. Vol. 6. New York, USA: Routledge.

Davila, Carl. 2009. "Fixing a Misbegotten Biography: Ziryāb in the Mediterranean World." Al-Masaq (Al-Masaq: Islam and the Medieval Mediterranean) 21 (2): 121–36.

Davis, Dick. 1995. The Shahnameh. New York, NY: Penguin Books.

Davis, Ruth F. 1992. "The Effects of Notation on Performance Practice in Tunisian Art Music." The World of Music 34 (1): 85–114.

———. 1996a. "Arab-Andalusian Music in Tunisia." Early Music 24 (3): 423–37.

———. 1996b. "The Art/Popular Music Paradigm and the Tunisian Ma'lūf." Popular Music 15 (3): 313–23.

———. 1997. "Traditional Arab Music Ensembles in Tunis: Modernizing Al-Turath in the Shadow of Egypt." Asian Music 28 (2): 73–108.

———. 2002a. "Baron Radolphe d'Erlanger." In The Garland Encyclopedia of World Music: Middle East, edited by Virginia Danielson, Scott Marcus, and Reynolds Dwight, 6:501–4. Routledge.

———. 2002b. "Patronage and Policy in Tunisian Art Music." In The Garland Encyclopedia of World Music: Middle East, edited by Virginia Danielson, Scott Marcus, and Reynolds Dwight, 6:505–13. New York, USA: Routledge.

———. 2002c. Review of Review of "The Maqam Music Tradition of Iraq" by Y. Kojaman, by Y. Kojaman. British Journal of Ethnomusicology 11 (1): 163–70.

———. 2004. Mā'lūf, Reflection on the Arab Musical Heritage. Lanham, Maryland, Toronto, Oxford: The Scarecrow Press.

Degirmenli, Emir. n.d. "Caron Fibre Turkish & Arabic Ouds." http://www.emirdegirmenli.com/en/ouds/carbon-fiber-turkish-arabic-ouds/.

D'Erlanger, Rodolphe. 1917. "Au Sujet de La Musique Arabe En Tunisie." Revue Tunisienne 24: 91–95.

Dinkjian, Ara. 2013. Conversations with Manol. CD. CD Baby.

Donaldson, George, ed. 1899. Catalogue of the Musical Instruments and Objects Forming the Donaldson Museum. London: Waterlow & Sons Ltd.

During, Jean. 1988. "Barbat." In Iranica Online. https://iranicaonline.org/articles/barbat.

———. 2005. Musiche d'Iran: la tradizione in questione. Translated by Giovanni De Zorzi. Milano: Ricordi.

El-Shawan, Salwa. 1980. "The Socio-Political Context of al-Mūsīḳa al-Carabiyyaii in Cairo, Egypt: Policies, Patronage, Institutions, and Musical Change (1927–77)." Asian Music 12 (1): 86–128.

———. 1984. "Traditional Arab Music Ensembles in Egypt since 1967: 'The Continuity of Tradition Within a Contemporary Framework'?" Ethnomusicology 28 (2): 271–88.

———. 1985. "Western Music and Its Practitioners in Egypt (ca. 1825–1985): The Integration of a New Musical Tradition in a Changing Environment." Asian Music 17 (1): 143.

Engel, Carl. 1870. Descriptive Catalogue of the Musical Instruments in the South Kensington Museum: Science and Art Department of the Committer of Council on Education, South Kensington Museum. By Carl Engel. Chapman & Hall.

———. 1874. A Descriptive Catalogue of the Musical Instruments in the South Kensington Museum: Preceded by an Essay on the History of Musical Instruments. London, Britain: George E. Eyre and William Spottiswoode.

Ensemble de Musique Classique Arabe de l'Université Antonine. 2005. Music of the Abbasid Era: The Legacy of Ṣafiy a-d-Dīn al-Urmawī. Inedit / MCM.

Erlanger, B.R. d'. 1930. La Musique Arabe. Vol. I. Paris, France: Paul Guethner.

Erlanger, Rodolphe. 1959. La Musique Arabe. Vol. 6. Paris, France:

Librairie Orientaliste Paul Geuthner.

Faccenna, Domenico. 1962. Sculptures from the Sacred Area of Butkara I (Swat, W. Pakistan). Italy: Istituto poligrafico dello Stato, Libreria dello Stato.

Farhat, Hormoz. 2004. The Dastgah Concept in Persian Music. Cambridge University Press.

Farmer, Henry George. 1929. History of the Arabian Music to the Thirteenth Century. London, UK: Reeves.

———. 1930. "The Origin of the Arabian Lute and Rebec." Journal of the Royal Asiatic Society 62 (4): 767–83.

———, ed. 1933. An Old Moorish Lute Tutor, Being Four Arabic Texts from Unique Manuscripts in the Biblioteca Nacional, Madrid (No. 334) and the Staatsbibliothek, Berlin (Lbg. 516). Glasgow, Scotland: Civic Press.

———. 1936. "Turkish Instruments of Music in the Seventeenth Century." Journal of the Royal Asiatic Society of Great Britain & Ireland 68 (1): 1–43.

———. 1937a. "The Lute Scale of Avicenna." Journal of the Royal Asiatic Society of Great Britain and Ireland, no. 2: 245–57.

———. 1937b. "Was the Arabian and Persian Lute Fretted?" Journal of the Royal Asiatic Society 69 (3): 453–60.

———. 1939. "The Structure of the Arabian and Persian Lute in the Middle Ages." The Journal of the Royal Asiatic Society of Great Britain and Ireland, no. 1: 41–51.

———. 1944. "The Music of 'the Arabian Nights.'" Journal of the Royal Asiatic Society of Great Britain and Ireland, no. 2: 172–85.

———. 1950. "Arabian Musical Instruments on a Thirteenth Century Bronze Bowl." Journal of the Royal Asiatic Society 82 (3–4): 110–11.

Feldman, Walter. 1996. Music of the Ottoman Court: Makam, Composition and the Early Ottoman Instrumental Repertoire. Berlin, Germany: VWB (Verlag für Wissenschaft und Bildung).

Ferdowsi, Abolqasem. 2016. Shahnameh: The Persian Book of Kings. Translated by Dick Davis. New York, USA: Penguin Classics.

Fétis, François-Joseph. 1869. Histoire Générale de La Musique. Vol. 2. Paris, France: Librarie Firmin Didot Frères.

Fleuret, Maurice. 1975. "L'Irak, Capitale Rennes. Deuxieme Festival Des Arts Traditionnels. Maison De La Culture De Rennes." La Nouvelle Observateur, April 21, 1975.

Franke, Daniël, and Eckhard Neubauer, eds. 2000. Museum Des Institutes Für Geschichte Der Arabisch-Islamischen Wissenschaften: Beschreibung Der Exponate. Frankfurt: Institut für Geschichte der Arabisch-Islamischen Wissenschaften an der Johann Wolfgang Goethe-Universität.

Gerson-Kiwi, Edith. 1970. "On the Technique of Arab Taqsim Composition." In Musik Als Gestalt Und Erlebnis: Festschrift Walter Graf Zum 65, edited by E. Schenk, 66–73. Vienna, Austria: H. Böhlaus Nachf.

Global Oud Forum. 2021. "The Global Oud Forum 2021 - Musical Notes." Abu Dhabi, UAE.

Gordon, Matthew. 2004. "The Place of Competition: The Careers of 'arib al-Ma'muniya and 'Ulayya Bint al- Mahdi, Sisters in Song." In Abbasid Studies: Occasional Papers of the School of Abbasid Studies in Cambridg, 6-10 July 2002, 61–81. Leuven, Belgium: Peeters Publishers.

Gordon, Matthew, and Kathryn A. Hain. 2017. Concubines and Courtesans: Women and Slavery in Islamic History. Oxford University Press.

Gordon, Matthew S. 2004. "The Place of Competition: The Careers of 'Arib Al-Ma'Muniya and 'Ulayya Bint Al-Mahdi, Sisters in Song." Abbasid Studies: Occasional Papers of the School of 'Abbasid Studies, Cambridge, 5–10 July 2002, 61–82.

———. 2017. "Abbasid Courtesans and the Question of Social Mobility." In Concubines and Courtesans: Women and Slavery in Islamic History, edited by Matthew S. Gordon and Kathryn A. Hain, 1:27–51. Oxford University Press.

Goshtigian, Mary. 1939. Taksim (Improvisation) and Sha'ki. Fresno, California: Library of Congress Archive of Folk Culture.

Grame, Theodore. 1972. "The Symbolism of the 'Ud." Asian Music 3 (1): 25–34.

Gramit, David. 1986. "I Dipinti Musicali Della Cappella Palatina Di Palermo." Schede Medievali, no. 10: 5–55.

Hackin, Joseph. 1923. Les Collections Bouddhiques (Exposé Historique et Iconographique); Inde Centrale et Gandhara, Turkestan, Chine Septentrionale, Tibet. Paris: Musée National des Arts Asiatiques Guimet.

Haines, John. 2001. "The Arabic Style of Performing Medieval Music." Early Music XXIX (3): 369–80.

Harris, Julian. 2018. "Composing with the Oud: Maqam, Ta'biriyya and the Iraqi Legacy." Ph.D. thesis, London: King's College.

Hassan, Qassim Sheherazade. 2001. "The Baghdad 'ūd School." In The New Grove Dictionary of Music and Musicians, edited by Stanley Sadie and John Tyrell, 12:550. London, UK and New York, USA: Macmillan.

Hassan, Schéhérazade. 2011. "Non-assistance à trésor en danger. À propos des archives sonores de Bagdad. Un témoignage." Cahiers d'ethnomusicologie. Anciennement Cahiers de musiques traditionnelles, no. 24: 191–204.

Hellwig, Friedemann. 1974. "Lute Construction in the Renaissance and the Baroque." The Galpin Society Journal 27: 21–30.

Hilarian, Larry Francis. 2007. "The Migration of Lute-Type Instruments to the Malay Muslim World." In Conference on Music in the World of Islam. Assilah, Morocco.

Hipkins, Alfred J. 1888. Musical Instruments: Historic, Rare and Unique. Edinburgh, Scotland: Adam and Charles Black.

Houssay, Anne and Wolfgang Früh. 2012. "Restauration d'une Kuitra Du Xixe Siècle." In Annual Meeting of the International Committee of Musical Instrument Museum and Collections CIMCIM 2011 – Tervuren Reports, 87–110. Tervuren: Royal Museum for Central Africa.

Imhof, Agnes. 2013. "Traditio Vel Aemulatio? The Singing Contest of Sāmarrā', Expression of a Medieval Culture of Competition." Der Islam 90 (1): 1–20.

International Council of Museums, Comité international des musées et collections d'instruments de musique, Meeting, and Musée royal de l'Afrique centrale. 2011. CIMCIM 2011, Tervuren: Reports, Annual Meeting of the International Committee of Musical Instrument Museum [i.e., Museums] and Collections = CIMCIM 2011, Tervuren: Rapports, Rencontre Annuelle Du Comité International Des Musées et Collections D'instruments de Musique. Tervuren, Belgium: Koninklijk Museum voor Midden-Afrika = Musée royal de l'Afrique centrale.

Invernizzi, Antonio. 1991. "De Hatra à Aïrtam: Frises Aux Musiciens." In Histoire et Cultes de l'Asie Centrale Préislamique: Sources Écrites et Documents Archéologiques, edited by Paul Bernard and Franz Grenet, 39–47. Paris, France: Centre National De La Recherche Scientifique.

Islay, Lyons, and Harald Ingholt. 1957. Gandhāran Art in Pakistan. New York, USA: Pantheon Books.

Jenkins, Jean, Poul Rovsing Olsen, and Horniman Museum. 1976. Music and Musical Instruments in the World of Islam. London, UK: World of Islam Festival Publishing Company Limited.

Johns, Jeremy. 2010. "Le Pitture Del Soffitto Della Cappella Palatina." In La Cappella Palatina a Palermo, 17:387–407. Mirabilia Italiae. Modena: Franco Cosimo Panini.

Jordi Savall, Hesperition XXI. 2009. Istanbul. Dmitrie Cantemir 1673–1723. Vol. IX. Raíces & Memoria. Alia Vox.

Jubrān, Kamīlyā. 2017. To make up for what we've lost: an interview with Kamīlyā Jubran. Interview by Hussein Al-Hujayri. Translated by F. Zahra. https://ma3azef.com/we-make-up-for-whatweve- missed-an-interview-with-kamilya-jubran/.

Kallimopoulou, Eleni. 2009. Paradosiaká: Music, Meaning and Identity in Modern Greece. Burlington, Canada: Ashgate.

Kassabian, Anahid. 2013. Ubiquitous Listening: Affect, Attention, and Distributed Subjectivity. Berkeley, USA: University of California Press.

Kennedy, Hugh. 2005. When Baghdad Ruled the World: The Rise and Fall of Islam's Greatest Dynasty. Massachusetts, USA: Da Capo Press.

Kerslake, Celia, Kerem Öktem, and Philip Robins, eds. 2010. Turkey's Engagement with Modernity: Conflict and Change in the Twentieth Century. Palgrave Macmillan.

Khaznadar, Chérif. 1998. "Munir Bashir, l'homme." Cahiers d'ethnomusicologie. Anciennement Cahiers de musiques traditionnelles, no. 11: 221–25.

Kilpatrick, Hilary. 2002. Making the Great Book of Songs: Compilation and the Author's Craft in Abû l-Faraj al-Isbahânî's Kitâb al-Aghânî. London: Routledge.

Kinzer, Joseph. 2016. "The Agency of a Lute: Post-Field Reflections on the Materials of Music." Ethnomusicology Review July.

Kinzer, Joseph M. 2017. "Bodies of Sound, Agents of Muslim Malayness: Malaysian Identity Politics and the Symbolic Ecology of the Gambus Lute." Ph.D. dissertation, University of Washington.

Kojaman, Y. 2001. The Maqam Music Tradition of Iraq. London: Y. Kojaman.

Lambert, Jean. 2010. "Le Musicien Yahyâ Al-Nûnû: L'émotion Musicale et Ses Transformations (Yémen)." Cahiers d'ethnomusicologie 23: 147–71.

———. 2021. "Which Lute Was Played in the Sawt of the Gulf Before the Twentieth Century?" In Music in Arabia: Perspectives of Heritage, Mobility and Nation, 87–106. Bloomington, Indiana: Indiana University Press.

Lane, Edward William. 1860. An Account of the Manners and Customs of the Modern Egyptians: Written in Egypt during the Years 1833, -34, and -35, Partly from Notes Made during a Former Visit to That Country in the Years 1825, -26, -27, and -28 ... the 5th Ed., with Numerous Additions and Improvements, from a Copy Annotated by the Author. Edited by His Nephew, Edward Stanley Poole. Edited by Edward Stanley Poole. 5th ed. John Murray.

Lavin, Gabriel. 2016. "Thinking Historically, Being Present: Kuwait, Summer 2016." Ethnomusicology Review October. https://ethnomusicologyreview.ucla.edu/content/thinking-historically-being-present-kuwait-summer-2016.

———. 2017. "The Oud at the Junction of the Nile." Oudmigrations. 2017. https://oudmigrations.com/2017/06/12/the-oud-at-the-junction-of-the-nile/.

Lowe, Michael. 1976. "The Historical Development of the Lute in the 17th Century." The Galpin Society Journal 29: 11–25.

Lundberg, Robert. 1992. "In Tune with the Universe: The Physics and Metaphysics of Galileo's Lute." In Music and Science in the Age of Galileo, edited by Victor Coelho, 211–39. Springer.

Lyons, Malcolm Cameron, and Ursula Lyons, trans. 2010b. The Arabian Nights. Tales of 1001 Nights: Volume 2. Penguin Classics. London: Penguin Books.

Maḥmūd, Guettat. 2006. Āla Al-'Ūd (The Instrument 'Ūd). Musqaṭ: Markaz 'Umān al-Mūsiqa at-Taqlīdiyya.

Marcel-Dubois, Claudie. 1941. Les Instruments de Musique de l'inde Ancienne. Vol. 11. Paris: Presses Universitaires de France.

Margoliouth, David Samuel. 1922.

The Table-Talk of a Mesopotamian Judge. London: Royal Asiatic Society.

Miller, Lloyd. 1999. Music and Song in Persia: The Art of Avaz. London: Curzon Press.

Mohafez, Arash. 2013. Ajamlar: An Anthology of Pieces by Persian Composers and Their Contemporaries at Ottoman Court from the 16th and 17th Centuries. CD. Tehran: Mahoor Institute of Culture and Arts.

———, ed. 2015. Compositions Attributed to Iranian Musicians in Ali Ufki and Dimitrie Cantemir's Collections. Tehran: Mahoor.

Monod, Odette. 1966. Le Musée Guimet. Collection Des Guides Du Visiteur. Paris: Guimet, Musée National des Arts Asiatiques.

Morra, Salvatore. 2017. "A Tunisian Musical Icon." Oudmigrations. 2017. https://oudmigrations.com/2017/05/28/a-tunisian-musical-icon/.

———. 2018. "The Tunisian 'ūd 'arbī: Identities, Intimacy and Nostalgia." Ph.D. thesis, London, UK: Royal Holloway, University of London.

Moukheiber, Karen. 2015. "Slave Women and Free Men: Gender, Sexuality and Culture in Early Abbasid Times." Ph.D. thesis.

———. 2019. "Gendering Emotions: Ṭarab, Women and Musical Performance in Three Biographical Narratives from 'The Book of Songs.'" Cultural History 8 (2): 164–83.

n.a. 1989. "Babylonian Culture Lives Again." St. Louis Post-Dispatch, September 18, 1989.

Nagoski, Ian. 2011. "To What Strange Place. The Music of the Ottoman-American Diaspora, 1916–29." (CD Liner Notes.). In To What Strange Place: The Music of the Ottoman-American Diaspora, 1916–29. San Francisco: Tomkins Square.

Najarian, Viken. n.d. "Electric Ouds."

Nassar, Issam, and Salim Tamari, eds. 2003. Al-Quds al-'uthmaniyya Fi Almudhakkirat al-Jawhariyya: Al-Kitab al-Awwal Min Mudhakkirat al-Musiqi Wasif Jawhariyya, 1904–1917 [Ottoman Jerusalem in the Jawhariyya Memoirs: Volume One of the Memoirs of the Musician Wasif Jawhariyya, 1904–1917]. Beirut: Institute for Palestine Studies.

Nettl, Bruno. 1992. The Radif of Persian Music: Studies of Structure and Cultural Context. Champaign, Ill.: Elephant & Cat.

Neubauer, Eckhard. 1993. "Der Bau Der Laute Und Ihre Besaitung Nach Arabischen, Persischen Und Türkischen Quellen Des 9. Bis 15. Jahrhunderts." Zeitschrift Für Geschichte Der Arabisch–Islamischen Wissenschaften 8: 279–378.

Newcomb, Anthony. 1986. "Courtesans, Muses, or Musicians? Professional Women Musicians in Sixteenth-Century Italy." In Women Making Music, edited by Jane Bowers and Judith Tick, 90–115. Springer.

Nielson, Lisa. 2012. "Gender and the Politics of Music in the Early Islamic Courts." Early Music History 31: 235–61.

Nielson, Lisa Emily. 2010. "Diversions of Pleasure: Singing Slave Girls and the Politics of Music in the Early Islamic Courts (661-1000CE)." Ph.D. thesis, University of Maine.

Nûnû, Yahyâ al-, and Jean Lambert. 2002. "L'autobiographie d'un Musicien Yéménite Traditionnel et Autodidacte?" Cahiers de Musiques Traditionnelles 15: 33–46.

O'Connell, John Morgan. 2016. Alaturka: Style in Turkish Music. 1st edition. London New York: Routledge.

Öktem, Kerem, Celia Kerslake, and Philip Robins, eds. 2010. Turkey's Engagement with Modernity: Conflict and Change in the Twentieth Century. St Antony's Series. Basingstoke: Palgrave Macmillan.

Othman Hassan, Karim. 2016c. "A Gem from Damascus, 1897." Oudmigrations. 2016c. https://oudmigrations.com/2016/05/30/a-gem-from-damascus-1897/.

———. 2016b. "An Oud in Layers." Oudmigrations. 2016b. https://oudmigrations.com/2016/05/10/an-oud-in-layers/.

———. 2016f. "Oud of a Luthiery Student." Oudmigrations. 2016f. https://oudmigrations.com/2016/03/11/oud-of-a-luthiery-student/.

———. 2016a. "Our Oldest Nahat." Oudmigrations. 2016a. https://oudmigrations.com/2016/03/09/our-oldest-nahat/.

———. 2016d. "Syrian Brothers in Istanbul." Oudmigrations. 2016d. https://oudmigrations.com/2016/05/16/syrian-brothers-in-istanbul/.

———. 2016e. "The Oldest Surviving Oud?" 2016e. https://oudmigrations.com/2016/03/05/770/.

Paniagua, Eduardo, Wafir Sheik, Jamila Ghalmi, and Luis Delgado. 1999. Jardín De Al-Andalus. Música Arabigo-Andaluza De La Sevilla Medieval. Vol. 120. Colección Al-Andalus. Pneuma.

Paniagua, Gregorio. 1977. Musique Arabo-Andalouse. Harmonia Mundi France.

Paniagua, Gregorio, Atrium Musicae, and ʿAbd al-Sadiq Shiqara. 1969. Monodia Cortesana Medieval (s. XII-XIII), Musica Arabigo-Andaluza (s. XIII). Hispavox.

Pasler, Jann. 2004. "The Utility of Musical Instruments in the Racial and Colonial Agendas of Late Nineteenth-Century France." Journal of the Royal Musical Association 129 (1): 24–76.

Pesuit, Margaret. 1997. "Representations of the Courtesan in Sixteenth-Century Venice: Sex, Class, and Power." Master's thesis, Montreal, Quebec: McGill University.

Picken, Laurence. 1955. "The Origin of the Short Lute." The Galpin Society Journal 8 (March): 32.

Pla, Roberto, and Arcadio de Larrea. 1969. Monodia Cortesana Medieval (s. XII-XIII), Musica Arabigo-Andaluza (s. XIII) [CD Liner Notes]. Hispavox.

Poché, Christian. 2000. "ʿUd." In The New Grove Dictionary of Music and Musicians. Oxford University Press.

Poor, Sara, and Jana Schulman, eds. 2007. Women and the Medieval Epic: Gender, Genre, and the Limits of Epic Masculinity. Palgrave Macmillan.

Prince-Eichner, Simone. 2016. "Embodying the Empire: Singing Slave Girls in Medieval Islamicate Historiography." Undergraduate, Pomona College.

Pugačenkova, Galina A. 1992. "New Terracottas from North Bactria." East and West 42 (1): 20.

Pugachenkova, G.A. 1979. Iskusstvo Baktrii Ėpokhi Kushan. Moscow: Iskusstvo.

Racy, A. J. 2004. Making Music in the Arab World: The Culture and Artistry of Tarab. Cambridge University Press.

Racy, Ali Jihad. 1976. "Record Industry and Egyptian Traditional Music: 1904–1932." Ethnomusicology 20 (1): 23.

———. 1981. "Music in Contemporary Cairo: A Comparative Overview." Asian Music 13 (1): 4.

———. 1991. "Historical Worldviews of Early Ethnomusicologists: An East-West Encounter in Cairo, 1932." In Ethnomusicology and Modern Music History, edited by Stephen Blum, Phillip V. Bohlman, and Daniel M. Neuman, 68–91. Urbana and Chicago: University of Illnois Press.

Rasmussen, Anne. 1992. "'An Evening in the Orient': The Middle Eastern Nightclub in America." Asian Music 23 (2): 63–88.

Rasmussen, Anne K. 1996. "Theory and Practice at the 'Arabic Org': Digital Technology in Contemporary Arab Music Performance." Popular Music 15 (3): 345–65.

———. 1997. "Made in America: Historical and Contemporary Recordings of Middle Eastern Music in the United States." Middle East Studies Association Bulletin 31 (2): 158–62.

Rasmussen, Anne K. 2021. "(Re)Patriating the Business of Music in Oman: Examples of the Tangible and

Intangible in an Omani Arts Economy." In Music in Arabia: Perspectives on Heritage, Mobility and Nation, 52–70. Bloomington, Indiana: Indiana University Press.

Renzovalle, P. Louis. 1913. "Un Traité de Musique Arabe Moderne," Mélanges de la Faculté Orientale, Beyrouth, no. VI: 1–120.

Reynolds, Dwight F. 2008. "Al-Maqqarī's Ziryāb: The Making of a Myth." Middle Eastern Literatures 11 (2): 155–68.

———. 2009. "The Re-Creation of Medieval Arabo-Andalusian Music in Modern Performance." Al-Masaq (Al-Masaq: Islam and the Medieval Mediterranean) 21 (2): 175–89.

———. 2017. "The Qiyan of Al-Andalus." In Concubines and Courtesans: Women and Slavery in Islamic History, edited by Matthew S. Gordon and Kathryn A. Hain, 100–123. New York: Oxford University Press.

Richardson, Kristina. 2009. "Singing Slave Girls (Qiyan) of the Abbasid Court in the Ninth and Tenth Centuries." In Children in Slavery through the Ages, edited by Gwyn Campbell, Suzanne Miers, Joseph C. Miller, 105–17. Athens, Greece and Ohio, USA: Ohio University Press.

Robertson, Bruce. 2004. "The South Kensington Museum in Context: An Alternative History."

Museum and Society 2 (1): 1–14.

Rohana, Nizar. 2021. "'Ud Taqsim as a Model of Pre-Composition." Ph.D. thesis, Leiden: University of Leiden.

Ronzevalle, P. L. 1907. "Un Traité de Musique Arabe- Préface, Traduction Française, Texte et Notes." In Mélanges de La Faculté Orientale, 1–120. Beirut, Syria: Université Saint-Joseph.

Roustom, Kareem Joseph. 2006. "A Study of Six Improvisations on the 'Ud by Riyad al-Sunbati." Master's thesis, Massachusetts, USA: Tufts University.

Rovsing, Miriam. 2002. "Contemporary Issues of Gender and Music." In The Garland Encyclopedia of World Music: Middle East, edited by Virginia Danielson, Scott Marcus, and Reynolds Dwight, 6:299–307. New York, USA: Routledge.

Royal Northern College of Music. 2010. Catalogue of the Collection: Collection of Historic Musical Instruments. Manchester: Royal Northern College of Music.

Sala, George Augustus. 1868. Notes and Sketches of the Paris Exhibition. Tinsley brothers.

Santore, Cathy. 1988. "Julia Lombardo," Somtusoa Meretrize": A Portrait by Property." Renaissance Quarterly 41 (1): 44–83.

Sawa, George Dimitri. 1985. "The Status and Roles of the Secular Musicians in the Kitāb Al-Aghānī (Book

of Songs) of Abu al-Faraj al-Iṣbahānī (D. 356 AH/967 AD)." Asian Music, 69–82.

———. 1989. Music Performance Practice in the Early 'Abbāsid Era 132-320 Ah/750-932 AD. Toronto, Ontario: Pontifical Institute of Medieval Studies.

———. 2019. Musical and Socio-Cultural Anecdotes from Kitāb al-Aghānī al-Kabīr: Annotated Translations and Commentaries. Brill.

———, ed. 2021. Ḥāwīl-Funūn Wa-Salwat al-Maḥzūn, Encompasser of the Arts and Consoler of the Grief-Stricken by Ibn al-Tahhan. Islamic History and Civilization 184. Leiden; Boston: Brill.

Seeman, Sonia Tamar. 2021. Sounding Roman: Representation and Performing Identity in Western Turkey. Oxford University Press.

Sezgin, Ekhart, ed. 1984. Zeitschrift Für Geschichte Der Arabisch-Islamischen Wissenschaften. Frankfurt, Germany: Institut für Geschichte der Arabisch-Islamischen Wissenschaften and Johann Wolfgang Goethe-Universität.

Shaw, Thomas. 1738. Travels, or Observations Relating to Several Parts of Barbary and the Levant: Illustrated with Cuts. The Theatre.

Shiloah, Amnon. 1972. La perfection des connaissances musicales. Traduction annotée du traité de musique arabe d'al-Ḥasan ibn Aḥmad ibn 'Ali al-Kātib. Place of publication not identified: LIBRAIRIE ORIENTALISTE PA.

———. 1995. Music in the World of Islam: A Socio-Cultural Study. Detroit, USA: Wayne State University Press.

Signell, Karl. 1977. Makam: Modal Practice in Turkish Art Music. Seattle, Washington: Asian Music Publications.

Smith, Eli, and Mikhail Meshakah. 1847. "A Treatise on Arab Music, Chiefly from a Work by Mikhail Meshakah, of Damascus." Journal of the American Oriental Society 1 (3): 173–217.

Söhne, Gerhard. 1994. "Zum Versuch Der Rekonstruktion Einer Frühen Arabischen Laute." Zeitschrift Für Geschichte Der Arabisch-Islamischen Wissenschaften 9: 357–72.

Stigelbauer, Michael. 1975. "Die Sangerinnen Am Abbasidenhof Um Die Zeit Des Kalifen Al-Mutawakkil Nach Dem Kitab al-Aghani Des Abu'l Farag al-Isbahani and Anderen Quellen Dargestellt." Ph.D. thesis, Universitat Wien.

Tamari, Salim, and Issam Nassar, eds. 2013. The Storyteller of Jerusalem: The Life and Times of Wasif Jawhariyyeh, 1904–1948. Northampton, Massachusetts, USA: Interlink Books.

Tannous, Alexandre. n.d. "Simon Shaheen: Talent, Charisma and Musical Identity."

Tarek, Abdallah. 2017. "L'art Du 'ūd Égyptien, de l'organologie à La Performance La Virtuosité Traditionnelle et Son Évolution à l'aune Du 78 Tours." Ph.D. thesis, Lyon: Université Lumière Lyon.

Targan, Sherif Muhiddin. 1995. Ud Metodu. Istanbul: Çağlar mûsiki Yayınları.

Tetik Isik, Seher. 2013. "The Works of Cafer Açin in Turkish Organology." Idil Journal of Art and Language 2 (6).

Tewfik, Nourhan. 2015. "Palestinian Singer and Oud Player Kamilya Jubran: 'My Repertoire Is My Story.'" Al Bawaba. 2015. https://www.albawaba.com/entertainment/palestinian-singer-and-oud-player-kamilya-jubran-my-repertoire-my-story-729914.

To What Strange Place. The Music of the Ottoman-American Diaspora, 1916–29. 2011. San Francisco: Tomkins Square.

Toker, Hikmet. 2012. "Sultan Abdülaziz Dönemi'nde Osmanli Sarayi'nda Mûsikî." Ph.D. thesis, Istanbul: Marmara Üniversitesi.

Tragaki, Dafni. 2009. Rebetiko Worlds. Newcastle: Cambridge Scholars Publishing.

Tripp, Charles. 2000. A History of Iraq. Cambridge: Cambridge University Press.

Tsuge, Gen'Ichi. 2013. "Musical Instruments Described in a Fourteenth-Century Persian Treatise 'Kanz al-Tuḥaf.'" The Galpin Society Journal 66: 165–259.

Tura, Yalçın. 2001. Kitabu 'İlmi'l-Musiki'ala Vechi'l-Hurufat, Musikiyi Harflerle Tesbit ve İcra İlminin Kitabı. Istanbul: Yapı Kredi Yayınları.

Türk Müzigi Ustalari. 2004. Ud: Türk Müzigi Ustalari. Kalan Müzik.

Ufki, Ali, and M. Hakan Cevher. 2003. Hâzâ Mecmûa-i Sâz ü Söz. Izmir: Meta Basım.

Ulaby, Laith. 2008. "Performing the Past: Sea Music in the Arab Gulf States." Ph.D. dissertation, Los Angeles: University of California.

Üngör, Etem Ruhi. 2000. "Geçmişten Günümüze: Türk Lütiyeleri." Musiki Mecmuasi, 2000.

Urkevich, Lisa. 2014. Music and Traditions of the Arabian Peninsula: Saudi Arabia, Kuwait, Bahrain, and Qatar. New York, USA: Routledge.

Van Edwards, David. 2011. "Arnault of Zwolle's Lute Design; a Puzzle Solved?" 2011. https://www.vanedwards.co.uk/month/dec11/month.htm.

Verrier, Luc. 2015. The Cairo Congress of Arab Music 1932. Paris: Bibliothèque nationale de France/Abu Dhabi Tourism & Culture Authority.

Villamont, Jacques de. 2012. Les Voyages Du Seigneur de Villamont. 1595 edition. Paris: ⊠Hachette Livre and BNF.

Villoteau, Guillaume André. 1813. "Première partie. Des instrumens a cordes connus en Egypte." In *Description historique, technique et littéraire des instruments de musique des Orientaux*. 221–246: Imperial Edition.

Wells, Elizabeth. 2007. "The Donaldson Collection in the Royal College of Music Museum of Instruments, London." *Musique. Images. Instruments: Revue Française D'organologie et D'iconographie Musicale Ix* 9: 103–25.

Wright, Owen. 1978. *The Modal System of Arabian and Persian Music, 1250–1300: An Interpretation of Contemporary Texts*. Vol. 28. London Oriental Series. Oxford, UK and New York, USA: Oxford University Press.

———. 2010. *Epistles of the Brethren of Purity: On Music: An Arabic Critical Edition and English Translation of Epistle 5*. London, UK: Oxford University Press.

———. 2018. *Music Theory in the Safavid Era: The Taqsīm al-Naġamāt*. London, UK: Routledge.

. 1992. Words without Songs: A Musicological Study of an Early Ottoman Anthology and Its Precursors. London, UK: University of London, School of Oriental and African Studies.

———. 1992b. *Demetrius antemir, the Collection of Notations. Volume 2. Commentary*. London: School of Oriental and African Studies, University of London.

Wulstan, David. 2009. "A Pretty Paella: The Alfonsine Cantigas de Santa Maria and Their Connexions with Other Repertories." *Al-Masāq* 21 (2): 191–227.

Zaimakis, Yiannis. 2021. "Music-Making in the Social World of a Cretan Town (Heraklion 1900–1960): A Contribution to the Study of Non-Commercial Rebetiko." *Popular Music* 30 (01): 1–24.

Zecher, Carla. 2000. "The Gendering of the Lute in Sixteenth-Century French Love Poetry." *Renaissance Quarterly* 53 (3): 769–91.

Zuhur, Sherifa, ed. 1998. *Images of Enchantment: Visual and Performing Arts of the Middle East*. Cairo, Egypt: American University in Cairo Press.

———. ed. 2001. *Colors of Enchantment: Theater, Dance, Music, and the Visual Arts of the Middle East*. Cairo: American University in Cairo Press.

———. 2003. 'Building a Man on Stage: Masculinity, Romance, and Performance According to Farid al-Atrash'. *Men and Masculinities* 5 (3): 275–94.

ENDNOTES

1. Writers relating the story include Hisham al-Kalbi (died ca. 819–821 CE), in Kitab al-Asnam; and Abu Talib al-Mufaddal (lived mid-ninth century CE), in Kitab al-Malahi.

2. The anonymous text was Kitab Kashf al-Humum; the man mentioned was called Abu al-Hasan al-Farabi.

3. This broad historical overview is drawn from Farmer (1929).

4. I continue to draw on Farmer (1929; 1930) in this overview.

5. Neubauer's translations and commentary on these sources underpin what I write in chapters 7-10 (Neubauer 1993).

6. "Equal temperament" is the system of tuning that spread around the world with keyboard instruments from the eighteenth century onwards. Technology has flattened out tunings, but these days it can also help us find the nuances of earlier traditions as alternatives. For example, benefitting from a mobile phone app that gives a range of possibilities, the Egyptian player Nehad Al Sayed tunes his oud according to Pythagorean pitch ratios.

7. One strange aspect of Meshakah's presentation is its apparent reversal of the strings, as if for a left-handed player (Abdallah 2017, 171).

8. The Musical Instrument Museums Online database is a good place to start discovering these. https://mimo-international.com/MIMO/

9. A full score transcription is available as a doctoral thesis: see Ufki and Cevher (2003).

10. The full score transcription is available: see Wright (1992a)

11. Vuslat in Recaizade Mahmud Ekrem's play Vuslat (literally, "The Lovers' Reunion," 1874), Dilber in Sami Paşazade Sezai's novel Sergüzeşt (Adventure, 1888), Meliha in Halid Ziya Uşaklıgil's story "Bir Yazın Tarihi" ("The History of a Summer," 1900), Müzehher in Saffet Nezihi's novel Zavallı Necdet (Poor Necdet, 1902), İsmet in Refik Halid Karay's novel İstanbul'un Bir Yüzü (One Face of Istanbul, 1920), and Zeynep in Halide Edip Adıvar's story "Zeyneb'im, Zeyneb'im" ("My Zeynep, My Zeynep"), which is included in the author's book Dağa Çıkan Kurt (The Wolf Who Climbed the Mountain, 1922).

12. "Munir hated microphones, he would always refuse amplification in his concerts"; Laurent Aubert, personal communication to the author, March 2019.